Fighting Fair

Along with used car dealers and telemarketers, lawyers are considered among the least trustworthy of all professionals. If lawyers want more respect, they will have to earn it by reframing their ethical responsibilities. In an original approach to law's moral dilemma, legal theorist Allan C. Hutchinson takes seriously the idea that 'litigation is war.' By drawing an extended analogy with the theory of ethical warfare, he examines the most difficult questions facing practicing lawyers today. Comparing the role of military officers to legal professionals and theories of just peace to legal settlement, Hutchinson outlines a boldly original approach to legal ethics.

Fighting Fair's recommendation for a more substantive, honor-based approach to ethics will be a thought-provoking tool for anyone concerned about the moral standing of the legal profession.

Allan C. Hutchinson is a distinguished research professor at Osgoode Hall Law School, York University in Toronto and an internationally recognized legal theorist. He is the author or editor of twenty books, including *Evolution and the Common Law* (2005), *The Province of Jurisprudence Democratized* (2008) and *Is Eating People Wrong?* (2010).

Fighting Fair

Legal Ethics for an Adversarial Age

ALLAN C. HUTCHINSON
Osgoode Hall Law School, York University

CAMBRIDGE
UNIVERSITY PRESS

CAMBRIDGE
UNIVERSITY PRESS

32 Avenue of the Americas, New York NY 10013-2473, USA

Cambridge University Press is part of the University of Cambridge.

It furthers the University's mission by disseminating knowledge in the pursuit of education, learning and research at the highest international levels of excellence.

www.cambridge.org
Information on this title: www.cambridge.org/9781107116917

First published 2015

A catalogue record for this publication is available from the British Library

Library of Congress Cataloguing in Publication data
Hutchinson, Allan C., 1951– author.
Fighting fair : legal ethics for an adversarial age / Allan C. Hutchinson, Osgoode Hall Law School, York University.
pages cm
Includes bibliographical references and index.
ISBN 978-1-107-11691-7 (hardback) – ISBN 978-1-107-53970-9 (pbk.)
1. Legal ethics. I. Title.
K123.H88 2015
174′.3–dc23 2015009568

ISBN 978-1-107-11691-7 Hardback
ISBN 978-1-107-53970-9 Paperback

A2J

For war is the hardest place: if comprehensive and consistent moral judgments are possible there, they are possible everywhere.

– Michael Walzer

Contents

Preface

As always, I have incurred a lot of debts in researching and writing this book. I gave lectures, seminars and talks at a number of law schools and conferences; the feedback was most helpful and constructive. As well, I have been teaching a first-year course over the past few years at Osgoode Hall, titled 'Ethical Lawyering in a Global Community'. I am grateful to my fellow instructors and to all the students in that course for pushing me on my ideas and giving me the opportunity to refine them.

Most importantly, I benefited greatly from conversations with Amaya Alvez, Lillianne Cadieux-Shaw, Richard Devlin, Adam Dodek, Trevor Farrow, Tiffany Herbert-Ramsubick, Cynthia Hill, Ian Langlois, Jennifer Leitch, Art Linton, Domingo Lovera, Chris MacCormack, Patrick Monahan, Derek Morgan, Hannah Ordman, Maria Panezi, Lorne Sossin, Samuel Sutherland and Emanuel Tucsa. Their critical assistance and intellectual support were invaluable. In researching and completing this project, I received a grant from the Social Sciences Research Council of Canada. That support has been indispensable.

Finally, I want to dedicate this book to my dad, who died soon after this book was completed. He lived a good and long life and set an example of what it is to fight fair.

May 2015

1

An Opening Salvo

It is a common trope that 'litigation is war.'[1] As an adjunct of the general adversarial structure and legal process, litigation is cast as a hostile encounter in which each party through its lawyers is entitled and recommended to use whatever lawful means are at its disposal to achieve victory. Within this bellicose depiction, lawyers are represented as frontline combatants who do battle on behalf of their clients. Championing the causes of their clients, their skill is found in their grasp of the techniques and strategies needed in this most intimidating and rarified of institutional venues. In this professional undertaking, they are licensed and often required to engage in activity that might at best be frowned upon if done in their personal lives and at worst even be condemned as deeply unethical. Although criticism of lawyers is far from new, it seems particularly insistent and widespread today: the extant modes of justification for the model of the 'ethical litigator' have been the subject of enormous criticism from both inside and outside the legal profession. The time is now ripe for change.

OPENING SHOTS

As lawyering (and, therefore, litigation) has become big business, the substantial price of entrepreneurial success has been bought at the perceived cost of reduced social standing. Lawyers are not

[1] As Lord Denning declared, 'in litigation as in war'. *Burmah Oil Co. v. Bank of England* [1979] 1 W.L.R. 473 (C.A.) [484] (Eng. and Wales). *See also* Jerome Frank, *Courts on Trial: Myth and Reality in American Justice* 8 (1959).

only portrayed as skilled at the dubious arts of manipulation and double dealing, but also castigated as moral hypocrites because they defend these practices in the brazen name of 'professional ethics'. Along with used car dealers and telemarketers, lawyers are considered among the least trustworthy and least respected of all professionals. The keen force of considered judgment is that many lawyers have failed to grasp the full ramifications of the crucial distinction between operating as a business and functioning as a profession. Lawyers have acted in ways that either ignore the public aspect of their professional status or, more cleverly, interpreted that public dimension as being consonant with the business interests of the profession. This is an ethical failure of considerable magnitude. In such a climate, it is not surprising that there are increasingly urgent calls for a more ethical practice of law as well as a more compelling theoretical account of legal ethics. In short, the legal profession is being asked to put its ethical money where its professional mouth is.

I will strive to suggest a more promising and less constrained approach to developing a defensible theory and practice of legal ethics. The problem is not simply that lawyers act in ways that are unethical, but that there is a failure to substantiate what it is to be an 'ethical lawyer' in the conditions of today's profession and society. Accordingly, the main thrust of my stance will be to contend that, if lawyers want to receive more professional respect for their work, they will have to earn it by reframing their ethical duties and taking them more seriously. Offering better explanations and more novel justifications for existing practices cannot do this.[2] Instead, it will require a genuine willingness to change what lawyers do and, as important, how lawyers think about what they do. There needs to be a sea change in the theory and practice of legal ethics and professional responsibility. As the 1996 Professionalism Committee of the American Bar Association Section of Legal Education and Admissions to the Bar concluded, 'the bottom line is that lawyer professionalism has declined in recent years and increasing the level of professionalism will require significant changes in the way professionalism ideals are taught and structural changes in the way law

[2] *See, for example*, W. Bradley Wendel, *Lawyers and Fidelity to Law* (2010).

firms operate and legal services are delivered.'[3] To date, that challenge has not been satisfactorily met.

One place to begin is by taking seriously the notion that 'litigation is war.' While this may seem an unpromising location, it has much to recommend it. Although it is often said that 'all's fair in love and war',[4] the fact is that all is not considered fair in war. There is a large and established body of work on military ethics that offers a sophisticated account of what it is to be fair and just in the commencement and prosecution of war. Even though the stakes may be higher on the battlefield than in the courts, it is telling that the discourse around the 'ethics of warfare' is much richer and more resourceful than that around legal ethics. Compared to their legal counterparts, military officers have available to them (and are obliged to comply with) a much more demanding set of ethical imperatives to construe and reflect on when pursuing their chosen profession.[5] Indeed, while it can still be reported that 'some sense of military honor is still the creed of the professional soldier',[6] such a conclusion is difficult to sustain fully in regard to the legal profession. Indeed, although there are many ethical lawyers, the profession as a whole seems not only to have lost much of its ethical luster, but also to have largely forsaken its claim to being an honorable undertaking of ethical integrity. Anthony Kronman is not so wide of the mark when he concludes that the contemporary 'practice of law [has lost] its status as a calling and degenerat[ed] into a tool with no more inherent moral dignity than a hammer or a gun'.[7]

3 Am. Bar Ass'n, Section of Legal Education and Admission to the Bar, Teaching and Learning Professionalism: Report of the Professionalism Committee 4–5 (1996).

4 John Lyly, *Euphues: The Anatomy of Wit* (1578).

5 *See* Peter S. Temes, *The Just War* (2003).

6 Michael Walzer, *Just and Unjust Wars: A Moral Argument with Historical Illustrations* XXV (3rd ed. 2000).

7 Anthony T. Kronman, *The Lost Lawyer: Failing Ideals of the Legal Profession* 364 (1993). *See also* David Barnhizer, *Golem, 'Gollum', Gone: The Lost Honor of the Legal Profession* 10 (Cleveland-Marshall College of Law, Working Paper no. 11–203, 2011), *available at* http://ssrn.com/abstract=1734412 ('There is a widespread impression that the practice of law has become primarily a money-grubbing, profit-maximizing, hustling business, rather than an admired profession.'). This stands in stark contrast to Tocqueville's roseate description of nineteenth-century lawyers. *See* 1 Alexis de Tocqueville, *Democracy in America*, 288 (Alfred A. Knopf ed., 1945) ('If I were asked where I place the American

Consequently, I want to recommend that it will be helpful to think about legal ethics in a way that is more consistent with and informed by the ethics of warfare.[8] While many lawyers and legal theorists might be tempted to look down their noses at 'military ethics', such an exercise has considerable potential to cast a fresh light on lawyers' professional responsibility and suggest fruitful ways to rethink how lawyers' ethical duties and professional conduct are conceived. Contrary to common wisdom, military engagement in war is a much more ethically regulated activity than litigation. In short, such a comparison between military and legal ethics might not only recommend new answers to old questions, but also stimulate a range of new questions for consideration. As such, this book offers itself as a salvage exercise: it takes foundational aspects of the existing legal system and process as a given (e.g., the adversarial system and the organizational economy of private practice) and then explores ways that the ideal of the ethical lawyer might be reimagined to advance better the best values and ambitions of such a system.

By way of general caveat, I concede that treating litigation as war is neither the best nor the most desirable characterization over the long haul. Litigation's conduct as a mode of guerilla warfare does not benefit the litigating parties and does little credit to lawyers' participation.[9] However, insofar as adversary ethics will continue to frame both litigation and its lawyering ethic in the foreseeable future, there is still much that can be done to improve the ethical quality and performance of litigation. Once it is understood that

aristocracy, I should reply without hesitation that it is not among the rich, who are united by no common tie, but that it occupies the judicial bench and the bar.').

[8] *See The Price of Peace: Just War in the Twenty-First Century* (Charles Reed & David Ryall eds., 2007). Others have noted the connection between legal ethics and military ethics, but to no great effect, development or influence. *See* David Luban, *Lawyers and Justice* (1988); *The Leader's Imperative* (J. Carl Ficarrotta ed., 2001); Anthony E. Hartle, *Moral Issues in Military Decision Making* (2nd ed. 2004). For more hands-on instruction in how to use military strategy for litigation purposes, *see, for example*, Frederick L. Whitmer, *Litigation Is War* (2007).

[9] The literature on the failings of litigation and the need for a more conciliatory structure and approach is vast. For a good introduction and intervention, *see* Julie Macfarlane, *The New Lawyer: How Settlement Is Transforming the Practice of Law* (2008).

'war' is not necessarily treated as a free-for-all in which there are no ethical precepts or principles in play, it might become possible for lawyers to take military ethics seriously and to learn from its study. As Walzer puts it, war is 'a world of permissions and prohibitions – a moral world'.[10] Consequently, this book seeks to demonstrate how military ethics can be fruitfully deployed as an analogical source for improving and deepening the theory and practice of legal ethics. Indeed, the sobering truth is that the discursive resources and frameworks for evaluating the ethical merit of military action are much richer and more sustaining than that of legal ethics.

A PLAN OF ATTACK

Throughout this book, my critical focus will be on how best to move forward the debate about the relationship between law, justice and legal ethics in a more rewarding and fulfilling direction. In the second chapter, I will revisit the general debate over the nature of the ethical project and how it plays out in the context of professionals; the focus will be on role differentiation and the demands placed on the legal profession in contemporary society. Third, I will look to the present state of theorizing in legal ethics; I highlight its failure to offer a sustaining or defensible restatement of professional responsibility. In the fourth chapter, I provide a sustained and broad-ranging critique of the hired-hand model of ethical lawyering; I suggest why a different approach drawing on military ethics offers genuine promise. Fifth, I survey the tradition of military ethics and make general comparisons between military officers and legal professionals; the emphasis is on both the strengths and weaknesses of such a comparison. In the sixth chapter, I start to explore the implications for legal ethics of the established principles for demarcating a war as just; this involves reassessing the current thinking on client selection and the decision to litigate. Seventh, I move on to the requirements of utilizing just means to prosecute a just war and recommend their relevance to legal practice; the effects on third parties and

[10] Walzer, *supra* note 6, at 36.

the role of junior lawyers are at the heart of the analysis. In the eighth chapter, I look to the recent literature on making a just peace and suggest how this might better guide lawyers in negotiating and reaching settlements. By way of conclusion, I drive home the beneficial consequences of viewing and refocusing legal ethics through the lens of military ethics.

2

The Professional Project

All societies have a set of moral standards by which they require or urge their members to abide. Although those standards might be more or less exacting in the obligations they impose and more or less observed in actual compliance, they do constitute an important dimension of social life. However, descriptive efforts to map the morality of any particular society are of limited value because they will reveal little about the important question of whether such morality is worthy of approval or adoption. Accordingly, it is necessary to develop a framework within which to evaluate conduct that is claimed to be morally defensible and also to confirm or deny its acceptability. This is the focus of ethical study.[1] At its broadest, ethics involves a meditation on what is wrong and right and, most important, on how such standards are arrived at and validated. Traditionally, the task was to elaborate and justify a set of ethical norms that provided an authoritative code that people could consult and follow in resolving difficult dilemmas. However, faith in the possibility of sketching such a body of enduring and universally valid rules has been waning. There is now the less absolutist and more skeptical acceptance that ethics is a situational practice that cannot claim objective or neutral justification in any genuinely strong or enduring way. As such, what is to count as a good moral reason is a matter of justification and persuasion, not proof and authority.

[1] For good introductory overviews, *see A Companion to Ethics* (Peter Singer ed., 1993); Roger Scruton, *Modern Philosophy* (1994). Throughout, I will give no particular weight to any distinction between the labels 'ethical' and 'moral'.

THE ETHICAL PROJECT

At bottom, ethics is about putting limits on the unhindered pursuit of self-interest. While there will be some overlap in particular instances between ethical justification and the advancement of self-interest, this is as much by coincidence as by design. The recognition and promotion of self-interest are not entirely inappropriate; people are not expected to be selfless or saintly in achieving ethical approval for all their actions. So, while people are entitled to weigh self-interest in the balance in reaching an ethically defensible line of conduct, they are not permitted to prioritize it without more. As such, an ethical schema that reduces only to the facilitation of individuals' self-interest is really no ethics at all.

Of course, an ethical code is not an exhaustive compendium of right answers and settled guidelines. While it often recommends bounds on acceptable conduct and seeks to distinguish good from bad behavior, it will operate more as a set of resources through which to think about and decide what to do than a corpus of pat answers to moral dilemmas. As such, the development of a sound ethical framework will not be devoted to listing a detailed roster of formulaic answers. Instead, it will be more concerned with generating a series of arguments and considerations – a discourse, if you will – that any person who seeks to act ethically can consult and weigh in deciding on a suitable course of action. Viewed in this way, a proposed ethics poses a series of orienting questions as much as it offers a compendium of authoritative answers. Accordingly, acting ethically is not about adherence to a code resorted to in occasional moments of indecision. Rather, it is about the development of a moral habit of living and acting that encompasses an organic set of attitudes, dispositions, assumptions, markers and values, and that can be incorporated into people's daily routines and regimens.[2]

In developing such an ethical scheme, it is important to appreciate the different phases and components of ethical behavior. These can be helpfully identified in a threefold format consisting of moral

[2] *See* Allan C. Hutchinson, *The Province of Jurisprudence Democratized* (2008). In the legal ethics context, *see* Don Nicolson & Julian Webb, *Professional Legal Ethics* (1999).

sensitivity, moral judgment and moral conviction.[3] Each of these interconnected stages of ethical deliberation needs to be appreciated by those who wish to understand and pursue an appropriate practice of ethical conduct:

- *Moral sensitivity* is the capacity to recognize that a situation has moral dimensions, that it presents a choice of possible responses and that its resolution may have implications, large and small, for all parties involved, including oneself.
- *Moral judgment* is an ethical assessment about what one ought to do and involves drawing on a rich understanding of role expectations, situational balance, likely consequences and moral integrity to justify a particular line of action.
- *Moral conviction* includes the self-discipline and perseverance to implement the decision by giving priority to the decided-on moral course of action over other values or goals (e.g., career advancement, personal relationships, hedonistic pleasures).

Developing these skills and values is a difficult challenge for most people in most situations. Few people spend a great deal of time understanding these demands or reflecting on their import. However, most people are obliged to negotiate this difficult ethical terrain in one way or another. To be an ethical person is not only about acting ethically, but also about thinking ethically. As T. S. Eliot phrased it, 'the last temptation is the greatest treason:/ To do the right deed for the wrong reason.'[4] While this might be an exacting and perhaps contested standard, it does point up the challenge of being an ethical person. It asks that people not only act ethically, but that they do so for what they or others claim to be the right reason. To be an ethical person is a frequently demanding, often perplexing and always continuing undertaking.

[3] I have borrowed the work of the cognitive psychologist James Rest and given it certain twists to fit the legal context. *See* J. Rest, 'Morality', in *3 Handbook of Child Psychology* 556 (Paul Mussen series ed., John H. Flavell & Ellen M. Markman eds., 4th ed. 1983); James R. Rest, *Moral Development* (1986); Muriel J. Bebeau, James R. Rest & Darcia Narvaez, 'Beyond the Promise: A Perspective for Research in Moral Education', 28(4) *Educ. Researcher* 18 (1999).

[4] T. S. Eliot, *Murder in the Cathedral* in The Complete Poems and Plays of T.S. Eliot 258 (1929). There is, of course, the converse conundrum of whether it is right to do the wrong deed for the right reason.

But, if developing these ethical qualities is a difficult challenge for ordinary people in their lives, it is doubly difficult for lawyers in their professional lives. Not only do lawyers have to cultivate these qualities and resources in their personal lives, but they also have to determine to what extent these might need to be varied in their professional roles and augmented or modified by a different set of ethical capabilities. If lawyers are to live up to their obligations to act as a morally motivated and morally directed group of respected professionals, they must nurture a mode of practice equal to that task. There has to be an element of reflection and conscientiousness in developing and implementing a professional modus operandi. As professionals and as individuals empowered through that professional status, lawyers must be constantly appreciative of the need to act ethically and responsibly.

Accordingly, unlike most other areas of social behavior, the practice of law needs to develop a sophisticated ethical framework that enables individual legal practitioners to grasp and comprehend the subtlety and sweep of the moral imperatives imposed by virtue of their public and professional lives. This might well be significantly different (or not) from those moral imperatives that might guide them in their private and personal lives. This is not to say that lawyers should or should even attempt to occupy two separate ethical universes, but that they should work to appreciate the competing pushes and pulls between the collective ethos that informs their professional lives and the one that guides their personal lives.

In examining lawyers' present and future efforts to regulate the ethical practices of lawyers, much is rightly made of the fact that legal practice is a professional pursuit; lawyers do not operate as individuals, but as part of a collective enterprise that exists to serve interests other than their own advancement and benefit. What distinguishes the work of lawyers from that of other groups is that not only do they possess a sophisticated structure of organization and a formalized learning process, but also that their efforts are generally claimed to be conditioned by a spirit of public service.[5]

[5] *See* Roscoe Pound, *The Lawyer from Antiquity to Modern Times* (1953); Talcott Parsons, 'A Sociologist Looks at the Legal Profession', in *Essays in Sociological Theory* 370 (rev. ed. 1958); Deborah Rhode, 'The Professionalism Problem', 39 *Wm. & Mary L. Rev.* 283 (1998).

The practitioner's self-interest is balanced and checked by a professional devotion to serving both the client's interests and the public good. It is this element of public-spiritedness that sets lawyers apart from other tradespersons and that warrants their privileges and powers as a self-regulating organization. Lawyers receive power and prestige by virtue of their professional status and must look beyond their own self-interest to warrant their continued bestowal.

As professionals, therefore, lawyers find their moral obligations extend beyond an exclusive concern with furthering their own individual interests and personal aspirations; they are expected, not simply encouraged, to put the public interest ahead of their own interests. Although what the public interest demands in general and in particular circumstances will be contestable, a reasonable sense of the public interest does strongly suggest that good lawyers are not simply successful ones. While facilitating the goals of clients and acting with a consistent degree of efficacy is an important measure of a lawyer's performance, it is far from being the only one or even the most important. How lawyers succeed and what they succeed at is as important as whether they succeed. At times, lawyers will have to give business considerations a distinct and even distant second place to ethical concerns in their decision making and practices. Indeed, there may well be occasions when lawyers will be required to act in a way directly contrary to their business interests. Put another way, a serious commitment to upholding a responsible legal ethics means that lawyers will have to be alert to the tempered and modified meaning that 'success' will have in their professional pursuits.

However, the legal profession has always come under very strong criticism from a wide range of sources for its increasing failure to appreciate this vital distinction between operating as a business and functioning as a profession. Although the chorus of criticism seems particularly strident and insistent in the present day, there has never been a golden age of lawyering.[6] The basic thrust of this persistent criticism has been that, while paying loud and frequent lip service

[6] *See* David Mellinkoff, *The Conscience of a Lawyer* (1973); Marc Galanter, 'The Faces of Mistrust: The Image of Lawyers in Public Opinion, Jokes, and Political Discourse', 66 *U. Cin. L. Rev.* 805, 810–16 (1998) (noting historical fluctuation of lawyer stature against a baseline of significant public dislike for attorneys).

to its moral mandate to give priority to the public interest ahead of all other values, the legal profession has frequently placed the private interests of its members ahead of those of the public. Much of the critical literature has riffed on the basic assertion that legal ethics is as much an ideology as a moral code; it clothes particular interests in an ensemble of ethical mandates that do little to inhibit the advancement of the profession's collective and personal self-interest. In short, the bottom-line judgment is that the legal profession 'differ[s] from trade unions only in [its] sanctimoniousness'.[7]

Consequently, any effort to preserve or salvage the professional reputation of lawyers must strive to integrate better the business and ethical dimensions of legal practice. Indeed, there must be a renewed and concerted effort to reclaim and rethink the nature of this public-spiritedness that is supposed to animate legal professional ethics. If this is not done, the consequences will be devastating for both the legal profession and society at large. If the practice of law is simply thought of as a business with no special public or moral obligations, it will lose its already tenuous claim to ethical leadership and responsibility. The legal profession will not only forfeit its prestige and be less honorable in its orientation and ambitions, but, more important, society will be the poorer for it and be ill-served by such a profession.

BEING PROFESSIONAL

Most lawyers often forget that the study of legal ethics is a branch of ethics generally; it is not a subject unto itself. As with general ethics, the prevailing standards of right and wrong do not exhaust ethical inquiry into legal professionals' behavior; those standards must themselves be subject to scrutiny and challenge. Nevertheless, having developed a personal sense of moral integrity, lawyers should have this sense reinforced rather than jeopardized by the need to subordinate personal values to professional goals.[8] To ask lawyers to abandon entirely their personal ethical values when they act as

[7] Eliot Freidson, *Profession of Medicine* 369 (1970). *See also* Kronman, *supra* ch. 1, note 7, at 370; Mary Ann Glendon, *A Nation Under Lawyers* 285 (1999); and R. Abel, *American Lawyers* (1999).

[8] *See* Susan G. Kupfer, 'Authentic Legal Practices', 10 *Geo. J. Legal Ethics* 33 (1996).

lawyers is both unrealistic and undesirable. However, this does not mean that there has to be a perfect and consistent melding between a person's own ethical commitments and her moral sense of herself as a legal professional. A certain role differentiation can be a legitimate and defensible part of any general ethical approach. When acting in a professional capacity, persons can (and occasionally must) make decisions and act in a way that might be different to what they would do in a personal and nonprofessional context. At times, this differentiation might result in a professional being asked and even obliged to act in a moral way opposed to their personal code of ethical conduct.

The idea of role differentiation can be illustrated by a couple of straightforward examples. Imagine that a person is committed as a matter of personal ethics to treating people equally and fairly. Such a person will endeavor to act consistently from one situation to another. Also, appreciating that what counts as 'equal' and 'fair' is contestable and not always obvious in particular situations (e.g., dealing with disadvantaged persons), it might also demand a serious appraisal of the limits of such an ethical commitment. Such a person will realize that seeking to act in such a way will often involve actions that might well be against that person's own self-interest. To act ethically throughout one's life will take a strong and self-conscious combination of sensitivity, judgment and conviction. As with much else, it will be the effort to follow such a course of thinking and acting and not merely the success of that effort that will be decisive.

However, as difficult as following through on that general ethical role might be, there will be circumstances in which such a broad mandate might bring into play other different and perhaps competing roles. For instance, when acting as a parent, existing ethical practices suggest that persons will not only be entitled to favor their children over others, but might in some circumstances feel obliged to do so. When acting as a university official, for example, ethically motivated persons might not only believe that they should not favor their children in seeking admission to the university, but they might feel ethically prohibited from being part of any decision about their children or from participating in the admissions process. In each of these cases, although the best ethical course to follow might be unclear and controversial, it is generally conceded that the role that a person occupies will legitimately influence how and why she decides to act.

This insight (i.e., what might seem right and proper in one situation will seem wrong and improper in another situation) has profound implications for the study and understanding of legal ethics. So informed, the central question for professional ethics, therefore, is what is there about the professional role in question that allows or demands a different set of ethical considerations to be in play than in a more general and personal context. Moreover, even if it is considered that such circumstances exist for role differentiation, this will not validate or excuse anything and everything that professionals do. For instance, while actors seem warranted in adopting a stark differentiation between their personal lives and the dramatic roles they inhabit, other professionals may not make such a stark differentiation so easily. This seems to be the case for lawyers and soldiers – what lawyers do in the name of the Rule of Law and what soldiers do in the name of war will not be permitted or excused by that fact alone.

The key challenge for lawyers and soldiers, therefore, will be to connect the reasons for any deviation from nonprofessional norms to the different set of ethical expectations in the professional setting. Professionals do not have carte blanche to do whatever suits them; they must tailor their ethical commitments to the precise contours of their professional situations. So understood, it will be accepted that the reasons for role differentiation will inform both the circumstances for its accepted occurrence and the nature of the ethical deviations allowed or required. Accordingly, there is no justification to mandate a wholesale abrogation of personal moral responsibility by professionals. However, there is an ethical justification for acting differently in a professional capacity not as something entirely divorced from a more general ethical orientation, but as part of one. As such, personal and professional ethics are related as part and parcel of the same normative family.

The bridge that joins personal and professional ethics is the notion of the 'public interest'. If there is to be a strong role differentiation in personal and professional matters, it must be demonstrated that, insofar as professional conduct falls short of personal ethical standards, it serves some larger understanding of the public interest, not only the self-interest of the professional as an individual practitioner or as a member of its communal group. In short, it is incumbent on a profession to ensure that the public interest is placed squarely and regularly at the forefront of professional concerns. There must be some compelling justification that allows or requires professionals to adopt a course of conduct that varies from that recommended by the generally accepted modes of ethical behavior in society. As such, if professionals are to be encouraged to 'do wrong' in order to be good professionals (i.e., engage in activity that, while considered unethical in nonprofessional settings, might be excused when done as a professional), then there needs to be a more fully developed and better account of what that professional role is, what the public interests are that warrant such a differentiation and what are the parameters of professional conduct.

Like general ethics, therefore, professional ethics is contextual: it involves particular people in particular situations making difficult decisions, with particular time constraints and imperfect information, and with particular consequences for particular people. And, of course, there is no context that allows people to fix once and for all their obligations and actions when acting in personal or professional roles. There are few right answers that stand outside any context or debate. The traditional understandings and expectations are nothing more (or less) than the accumulated practices of professionals that have been affixed with institutional authority. However, attachment to a professional ethos means more than simply complying with extant laws, in both spirit and letter; this is a floor that all people must stand on. Professionals must obviously do this; professional morality is more than a law-abiding conformity. But, if they are to achieve the coveted status of genuine professionals, they must live up to a set of values and commitments that go beyond basic lawful deportment and that, instead, contribute to a defensible definition of the 'good professional'. It is in many ways a more, not less, demanding task to meet that professional ethical image than that faced by the ordinary person.

THE ETHICAL LAWYER

Lawyering is not simply another business. While lawyers are in business and entitled to maximize its profitable potential, they are members of a legal profession. As such, lawyers receive special privileges because they serve much broader public goals than their own private interests; lawyering has an indispensable public dimension that sets it aside from other businesses. In this context, 'good lawyers' are not simply those who reap substantial material benefits from their practice of law. While there is a disturbing tendency to equate the level of professional accomplishment with the extent of material reward, this measure is misleading. Many lawyers maintain the highest level of professional competence and achievement, but are relatively poorly paid for their services. Instead, successful or good lawyers are (or should be) better understood as those who maintain the highest standards of professional performance whether they are paid large or small sums for their efforts. To be a successful or good lawyer, therefore, demands a certain quality of ethical performance that in important ways serves the public interest.

When it comes to lawyers, therefore, the extent and nature of the differentiated professional role is to be determined by reference to 'the public interest'. Of course, this is a contested enterprise; there is no uncontroversial or obvious account available of what is in the public interest. What counts as the public interest and how it is translated into the more prosaic routines of practicing lawyers will determine by and large the ethical reputation and worth of lawyers. Although there are different views about the nature of this public interest, there is a relatively clear and shared norm that underwrites the work and privileged position of lawyers in most societies – it is a commitment to the Rule of Law. For instance, under the *Ontario Law Society Act*, the legal profession is granted certain functions, duties and powers on the condition that they are exercised 'to maintain and advance the cause of justice and the rule of law' and 'to facilitate access to justice for the people'.[9] Consequently, the legal profession is considered to have an overriding obligation to ensure not only that these public values are used to determine the

[9] Law Society Act, R.S.O. 1990, § 4.2 (Can. Ont.).

professional and ethical responsibilities of lawyers, but that they will inform and curtail the pursuit of other goals and ends.

In part, this crucial task can be achieved by improving the ethical framework offered by the rules of professional conduct and by enforcing them with greater vigor and seriousness. However, any serious look at such rules of professional conduct reveals that they are long on general exhortation and short on detailed guidance for lawyers. Perhaps this is no bad thing; it gives further credence to the general claim that ethical rules are less a set of directives from which professionals can draw precise direction than an institutionalized collection of practical wisdom by resort to which lawyers can engage and contest the nature of ethical obligation in professional situations and contexts.[10] That being the case, it becomes imperative to identify and scrutinize the dominant model of the ethical professional lawyer that underpins those rules and that shapes the ethical lives of lawyers. The ethical rules of legal professionals are animated and given substance by this underlying image of the 'good professional'.

Accordingly, any understanding of lawyers' professional role and conduct must address the adequacy of the model that underlies and frames lawyers' self-image as ethical professionals. In particular, this inquiry will follow two broad paths. The first concerns the neglected matter of whether the dominant model of ethical lawyering and its accompanying discourse are capable of assisting lawyers in nurturing the essential professional attributes of moral sensitivity, moral judgment and moral conviction. The second looks to whether this traditional approach supplies the best available means through which to serve the public interest by protecting the Rule of Law and access to justice. Taken together, these constitute the central challenge for the development and defense of a workable and fulfilling legal ethics: *Does the traditional approach offer the kind and extent of conversational resources that contemporary lawyers need to debate and determine the kind of legal professionals they should be?*

[10] *See generally*, Symposium, 'Critical Theories and Legal Ethics', 81 *Geo. L.J.* 2457 (1993); Symposium, 'Teaching Legal Ethics', 58 *Law & Contemp. Probs.* (Summer/Autumn 1995).

The ethical gauntlet was thrown down a long time ago in this particular debate. In a passing aside, Thomas Macaulay asked 'whether it be right that a man should, with a wig on his head, and a band round his neck, do for a guinea what, without these appendages, he would think it wicked and infamous to do for an empire'.[11] He was obviously implying that the putative gap between lawyers' personal and professional ethics was not 'right' and that legal ethics was severely wanting. While Macaulay may well have had a point about the traditional image of the ethical lawyer, his accusatory condemnation is too sweeping as it stands. The fact that there is a dissonance between the two is not the problem. Almost everyone would agree that there is an entirely justifiable account of why lawyers might (and occasionally perhaps 'should' or even 'must') act differently in their professional as opposed to personal capacity.[12] As Macaulay phrases it, it might be 'right' that such a discrepancy exists. The more telling issue is what particular differences should be countenanced. It will be essential to demarcate and explain which acts that are thought 'wicked and infamous to do for an empire' might be acceptable or even desirable for lawyers, wigged or otherwise, to do and which are not. This is a more selective and sophisticated challenge.

That being said, it is my contention that the discursive resources of the traditional approach to ethical lawyering are deeply and sorely lacking; they are wholly inadequate to the task asked of them. While the traditional approach insists on and demands a sharp division between lawyers' personal and professional ethics, it does so without subtlety or substance. Because it fails to explore sufficiently exactly why there is the need for such a separation, it

[11] Thomas Babington Macaulay, *Critical and Historical Essays Contributed to the Edinburgh Review* 312 (1877). A more modern rendition is: 'if a good professional must be a bad man, then it is immoral to be a good professional.' Arthur Isak Applbaum, *Ethics for Adversaries: The Morality of Roles in Public and Professional Life* 40 (1999). Applbaum concludes that the traditional rationales for the moral defensibility of adversarial actions do not hold analytical water; an immoral or false argument remains so whether it is made by a private person or a professional.

[12] *See, for example*, David Luban, *Lawyers and Justice* 145 (1988) ('The criminal defense lawyer ... will often find that the justifications of the role are so crucial that they override all but the most stringent demands of common morality.').

has little to contribute to the crucial debate about the scope, the content and the details of that partition. Indeed, the traditional framework runs out at exactly the point when lawyers most need some set of conversational resources by which to identify and help resolve the conundrums of how to be a good legal professional in modern society. Lawyers are left to their own devices to negotiate the intricate maze of ethical dilemmas – who to represent, how to represent them, how to appreciate the broader consequences of their work and so forth – in which they often find themselves. Rather than offer some ethical map and moral compass for those occasions when the professional rules are silent or offer conflicting assistance, the traditional model is content to suggest that whatever is lawful is also ethical. This is a cop-out of the first order; it hollows out legal ethics and makes professional responsibility a redundant notion.

The challenge, therefore, for lawyers both individually and collectively is to develop a mode of practice that can be justified in terms of this more public dimension of professional responsibility. This effort has centered on developing a style and substance of professional conduct that negotiates the difficult ethical space between the pull of general moral considerations and the push of a specialized professional role : How can lawyers be good professionals as well as good citizens? The traditional response has been to construct a 'differentiated role': lawyers might be entitled or even required to do things considered otherwise unethical in nonprofessional contexts. Clients are perceived to be autonomous in determining their own best interests and lawyers are expected to advance those interests with unconditional vigor, unquestioning loyalty, genuine candor and marked partisanship. Portrayed as super-technocrats, lawyers serve the legal system best and fulfill its broader goals of justice when they judge neither the moral worthiness of their clients nor the justness of their causes.

The difficulty with such a traditional model is that it can often lead to lawyers acting as the pilloried caricatures of common perception. They massage rules, distinctions, meanings and facts to serve their clients' purposes. Indeed, on extreme occasions, they might well be empowered to lie (i.e., asserting false statements) and cheat (i.e., advancing unreasonable and unverifiable claims and defenses) on behalf of their clients.[13] Under the traditional account of legal ethics, personal vices might well be tolerated or even celebrated as professional virtues. This is a far from edifying, let alone inspirational account of legal ethics and professional responsibility.

CONCLUSION

There is an urgent need, therefore, to remedy this situation and begin to re-envisage a model of the 'good lawyer' that better meets the needs of society and the legal profession in their quest to nurture and sustain ethical lawyers. The first step in doing that is to provide a more substantial and critical account of the limited imagery that underpins and energizes the traditional approach. This can be accomplished by unpacking and examining critically a state-of-the-art contribution to the theoretical debate in the form of a defense of the traditional model of lawyering. Only after that will it be possible to explore alternative images of the ethical lawyer.

[13] For a sophisticated account of this traditional role, *see, for example*, Sharon Dolovich, 'Ethical Lawyering and the Possibility of Integrity', 70 *Fordham L. Rev.* 1629 (2002) and Trevor Farrow, 'Sustainable Professionalism', 46 *Osgoode Hall Law Journal* 51 (2009). The origins and justification of this image are very much tied in with the operation of the criminal trial process. Indeed, if there is any ethically compelling purchase for this model, it is to be found in the role of criminal defense counsel. *See* Monroe H. Freedman, *Lawyers' Ethics in an Adversary System* 9–24 (1975) and David Layton, 'The Criminal Defence Lawyer's Role', 27 *Dal. L.J.* 379 (2004).

3

A Theoretical Excursion

In a prevailing climate of ethical ambivalence and professional indifference, it is not surprising that there are increasingly urgent calls for action. There are insistent demands for a more ethical practice of law as well as a more compelling theoretical account of legal ethics. In short, the legal profession is being asked to put its ethical money where its professional mouths is. An important and revealing attempt to do this is Bradley Wendel's *Lawyers and Fidelity to Law*. In a state-of-the-art and superior example of existing scholarship on legal ethics, the book offers itself as an ambitious effort to 'bridge the gap between academic philosophy (moral, political, and legal)...and the circumstances of actual practicing lawyers' and to provide a justificatory account of legal ethics that is 'about political legitimacy, not justice or ordinary morality'.[1] However, like most defenses of traditional approaches to legal ethics, Wendel's actual performance is exceeded by his general ambition. As such, its goal and its recommendations are emblematic of the general failure of contemporary thinking about legal ethics and professional responsibility.

In his acclaimed scholarship, Wendel has not so much offered a new approach to legal ethics as offered an *apologia* for extant professional practices. The fact that he has done so with jurisprudential sophistication and technical subtlety merely compounds the offense. His extended analysis manages to reveal, not retrieve the parlous state of legal ethics. Consequently, in examining

[1] W. Bradley Wendel, *Lawyers and Fidelity to Law 15 and 2* (2010).

Wendel's work, I offer two series of challenges to his justificatory theory of legal ethics – the first is jurisprudential and will expose the theoretical footings and failings of his account; the second is more practical and will look to its troubling implications for professional practice. In so doing, my critical focus will also be twofold – to demonstrate the limitations of present thinking and to suggest how best to move forward the debate about the relationship between law, justice and legal ethics. As the best and most celebrated piece of theoretical reflection in the area, Wendel's account is the perfect target for a critique of both the theory and practice of legal ethics. So goes Wendel, so goes contemporary scholarship.

A FAITHFUL INTERVENTION

Wendel's self-imposed task is not to design an entirely new model of ethical lawyering, but to offer a more compelling justification of existing practices. He is up-front in stating that his aim 'is to provide moral and political arguments for a version of... the Standard Conception of legal ethics'.[2] By this, he means that he takes the governing principles of client partisanship, substantive neutrality and non-accountability as the appropriate ethical indicators of good legal practice; lawyers act morally when they accept clients' interests without judging them and without responsibility for so representing them provided that they do so by legal means – morality equals legality, no more and no less. Wendel's hallmark contribution is to claim that, by offering a slight twist to the Standard Conception, it is possible to propose a much more cogent and complete justification of existing models and modes of legal professional conduct. It is a bold initiative.

Although the Standard Conception model recommends that lawyers take an amoral or a conscience-off stance in fulfilling their professional duties, Wendel devotes himself to defending this provided that it is interpreted to mean that lawyers 'protect the legal

[2] *Id.* at 6. Wendel's work is part of a recent revival in defending the Standard Conception of legal ethics. *See, for example*, Daniel Markovits, *A Modern Legal Ethics: Adversary Ethics in a Democratic Age* (2009) and Tim Dare, *The Counsel of Rogues?: A Defence of the Standard Conception of the Lawyer's Role* (2009).

entitlements of clients, not advance their interests'.[3] This entails lawyers accepting that their role is not to manipulate law to serve better their clients' interests, but to respect the law and to do what they can for their clients within this ethical horizon. In short, lawyers are to be vigorous partisans for their clients' interests as long as it is based on an underlying ethical duty 'to treat the law with respect, not merely as an inconvenient obstacle to be planned around'. Once understood in this way, Wendel maintains, this will be sufficient to give the lawyers' traditional modus operandi the imprimatur of ethical propriety: 'as long as the lawyer acts within the law, her actions may not be evaluated in ordinary moral terms.' Indeed, he goes so far as to insist that 'the lawyers' job is to push right up to the boundaries of the law,' but no further.[4]

Having made this small, but important modification to the Standard Conception, Wendel moves to his primary task of putting forward a more convincing defense of such a neo-traditional take on legal ethics. His most distinctive move is to insist that most legal ethicists have been barking up the wrong justificatory tree. For him, rather than make the futile effort to square legal ethics with the demands of general moral norms, it is necessary to reference the arguments and sources of deeper political theory: 'ethical justification of lawyers is not case-by-case, but systemic and institutional in nature' and 'legal ethics should be understood as part of the morality of communities.'[5] Once seen in this light, the traditional account of a strongly differentiated role between personal and professional ethical commitments is thought to be not only much more understandable, but also entirely defensible. The ethical warrant for legal professional conduct is located in political theory, not ethical theory. Wendel puts his faith in the ethical lawyer's commitment to be a loyal stalwart of the legal system.

Within a society that commits itself to the Rule of Law – 'legality is fundamentally a political value' – and its institutional imperatives,[6] Wendel asserts, individuals are entitled to rely on the full range of legal rights and entitlements in their dealings with the government

[3] *Id.* at 6 (emphasis in original).
[4] *Id.* at 3, 29 and 82.
[5] *Id.* at 7 and 41.
[6] *Id.* at 6.

and each other. The law represents the best compromise of competing values in a pluralistic society. And, because law is a validated product of democratic procedures, there exists an obligation to respect, if not necessarily to obey the law: 'lawyers must treat law as a reason for action as such, not merely a possible downside to be taken into account.'[7] Moreover, if law is worthy of respect, then lawyers who follow and show fidelity to law in their professional behavior should also be considered to act worthily.

Wendel's justificatory account of legal ethics, therefore, draws on a markedly positivist account of law's nature that builds on the work of both Herbert Hart and Joseph Raz. On such a view, law can be identified as a matter of fact through its social sources, not its political wisdom or moral value.[8] In this way, in going about their law-respecting business, 'the role of the lawyer is a morally respectable one,' even though it mandates lawyers not to look to general or ordinary moral considerations for guidance in their professional pursuits; professional ethics are politically related to, but not reducible to ordinary morality. So depicted, ethical lawyers can appeal to the legal system 'as an excuse for what would otherwise be deemed wrongful conduct'.[9]

Wendel warns that, in fulfilling its vital political role, the legal profession should not put its own professional interests or its interpretation of the public interest ahead of the citizenry that it is intended to serve. Lawyers' commitment is to the legal system and 'calling upon lawyers to interpret the content of law with respect to the public interest has the effect of reintroducing the normative controversy that the law is meant to settle.' Within such a justificatory framework, it would be unjust and indefensible if lawyers did more or less than ensure that people can access and activate their legal rights. For Wendel, therefore, not only is there no need for lawyers to act in solidarity with their clients' stance, but there are also important political reasons why lawyers should remain studiedly indifferent to their clients' causes and goals. By anchoring

[7] *Id.* at 49.

[8] In short, he goes with the 'softer' Hart on moral incorporation, but the 'harder' Raz on obligation and authority. *See* H. L. A. Hart, *The Concept of Law* (2nd ed. 1994) and J. Raz, *The Authority of Law* (1979).

[9] *Supra*, note 1 at 49, 10 and 26.

legal ethics in political morality rather than in common moral values, lawyers are expected to exhibit and embody 'fidelity to law' in their individual and collective actions. So, 'if a lawyer manipulates the law to obtain an unjust result, the proper basis for ethical criticism is failure to exhibit fidelity to law, not the resulting injustice.'[10]

This is an original and provocative account of legal ethics. Prepared to follow through on the basic logic of this jurisprudential stance, Wendel concludes that 'lawyers can lawfully do no more, *and should do no less*, than their clients are legally entitled to do.' So forcefully put, it is a demanding and uncompromising ethics. He not only views legal constraints as the floor of lawyering (as almost all lawyers and ethicists do), but also makes them its ceiling as well; lawyers are not only permitted to do anything that is legal, but are politically required to do so at their clients' behest. Unhindered by situational or local moral dilemmas, Wendelian lawyers can and should go about their robust advocacy on behalf of any and all clients 'without any moral qualms'. Under his political account of legal ethics, it becomes the ethical duty of lawyers to 'subordinate' or 'exclude' ordinary moral concerns from their professional resources or consideration.[11]

The central problem with Wendel's offering, though, is that, for all its erudition and elegance, it is not so much an account or justification of legal ethics, but almost a denial that lawyering is an ethical undertaking. There is no place for ethics in his political manifesto of professional lawyering. There is simply the institutional demand that lawyers make good faith efforts to interpret what the law is in any particular instance in a reasonable manner. This seems to be such a minimalist and open-ended injunction – *be reasonable* – as to allow lawyers to do not only almost whatever they want in the name of responsible professional behavior, but also to receive the stamp of ethical approval. Consequently, Wendel's prescription for the ethical malaise of contemporary legal ethics not only kills the patient, but also actually seems intended to do so. Under his scheme of legal ethics, there is little to discuss or wrestle with when it comes to acting professionally. If this engagement is a mark of

[10] *Id.* at 210 and 9.

[11] *Id.* at 168, 186, 155 and 157.

ethical conduct (as I will argue it is), then Wendel has nothing to tell us. For him, the professional dilemmas of legal ethics can best be handled by proceeding as if they did not exist.

In order to focus my critique and to delve a little deeper into Wendel's arguments, I will organize my comments around three particular issues – the mushy methodological foundations of his approach; the ethical vagueness of a 'good faith' constraint; and the interpretive difficulties in giving any practical bite to his proposals.

A JURISPRUDENTIAL RESPONSE

First, as a preliminary philosophical matter, Wendel signals that he intends to validate his account of legal ethics by a general reliance on 'wide reflective equilibrium'.[12] Whether viewed as a mode of epistemic justification or as a more pragmatic device, the methodological resort to reflective equilibrium calls in aid a to-and-fro deliberative process: moral intuitions or practices and theoretical principles are sought to be brought into temporary balance through adjustment and modification. In the field of legal ethics, this means that Wendel strives to work the methodological space between 'theoretical considerations and the actual norms followed by conscientious lawyers in their professional lives'. Accordingly, he moves between his theoretical commitment to a political morality of 'fidelity to law' and the Standard Conception of ethical lawyering in order to strike on a slightly revised account of legal ethics that best mediates the pushes of abstract philosophical principle and the pulls of practical professional practice. The result is his neo–Standard Conception based on the central imperative to 'protect the legal *entitlements* of clients, not advance their interests'.[13]

The obvious limitation with this way of proceeding is that extant practices and intuitions are given ethical weight in the justificatory method simply by virtue of their existence; there is no critical threshold to cross before they are taken seriously as valid

[12] *See* John Rawls, *A Theory of Justice* (2nd ed. 1999) and T. M. Scanlon, 'Rawls on Justification', in *The Cambridge Companion to Rawls* 139–67 (S. Freeman ed., 2002).

[13] *Supra*, note 1 at 15 and 6.

or credible ethical resources.[14] In Wendel's account, therefore, the initial reliability or deservingness of existing professional practices and intuitions about what is ethical for lawyers is taken for granted – 'the actual norms followed by conscientious lawyers in their professional lives'.[15] As such, the present approach to legal ethics in the form of the Standard Conception is open to minor realignment or recalibration, but little more.

But this seems to beg the very question that should be at the heart of the ethical inquiry into the professional practices of lawyers: Are existing models and understandings of the approved practice of professional lawyering, no matter how 'conscientious' lawyers consider themselves, worthy of moral standing? While the answer to that might be in the affirmative, this cannot be assumed without more. Wendel must offer some basic and independent defense of existing norms and demonstrate how they are not systematically skewed or perverse. Without more, he is engaged in a very narrow and circular exercise of defining 'conscientious' by reference to whatever most lawyers do. He assumes that which he claims to be justifying; it is a classic boot-strapping enterprise. Yet any effort at such justification is entirely beyond his foundational commitment to a hands-off positivist account of law and lawyering.

Second, at the dynamic heart of Wendel's recommendation is the claim that 'the fundamental ethical obligation of lawyers is fidelity to law.' As such, the primary and perhaps only constraint in play in assessing lawyers' conduct is whether they have interpreted in a reasonable and good faith manner what the clients' legal entitlements are. Drawing on his more general positivist account of why lawyers should respect law, he hangs his ethical hat on the claim that 'the value of legality makes it wrong to engage in excessively "creative and aggressive" interpretations of legal norms when advising clients or structuring transactions.' However, even this negligible constraint is relaxed in litigation that Wendel distinguishes from non-litigation work, such as transactional or drafting activity. He contends that there is greater leeway for idiosyncratic or dubious

[14] *See, for example,* Norman Daniels, *Justice and Justification: Reflective Equilibrium in Theory and Practice* 21–46 (1996).

[15] *Supra,* note 1 at 15.

interpretations in litigation because a third party (i.e., judge or adjudicator) is designated to take institutional responsibility for the law's ultimate and authoritative meaning.[16]

For Wendel, therefore, the lawyers' range and style of conduct derive from their efforts to make sense of pertinent legal rules or principles in a conscientious way. Recognizing that the law is not entirely determinate and is open to varying interpretations, the requirement of good faith interpretation is less about legal rightness and more about political reasonableness. This is all well and good as a general and abstract constraint on lawyers' conduct, but it seems entirely unsuited to the massive task – justifying the whole edifice of legal ethics – that it is supposed to perform.

For starters, Wendel needs some reliable and reasonably fixed standard by which to define 'good faith'. Like all the usual sweeping terms of professional codes like 'integrity' or 'honor', it defies easy or uncontroversial exposition. Grounding an ethics of lawyering in such a term is to put the entire operation on an unstable footing from the get-go.[17] The major responsibility of any workable account of ethical behavior is to supply some guidance or structure to debates about dealing with hard cases. Of course, it would be unfair and miss the point of ethical theory to expect Wendel to offer some formulaic advice that can be depended on to dispose satisfactorily of recalcitrant ethical dilemmas. But it is surely reasonable to ask for some better measure of ethical conduct than that it is simply done conscientiously. Indeed, Wendel's proposal seems even more baffling when it is understood that one of his main reasons for abandoning conventional ethical theory is that it offers instruction on right and wrong that is too contested and indeterminate: 'people are likely to disagree in good faith about how to specify an abstract ethical value as a concrete maxim of action.'[18] It is far from clear why legal interpretation should fare any better. Indeed, even a

[16] *Id.* at 178, 117 and 70–2.

[17] For my own efforts to explore 'good faith' in the adjudicative context, *see* Allan C. Hutchinson, *It's All in the Game: A Non-foundationalist Account of Law and Adjudication* 180–215 (2000). Indeed, when it comes to judging, it is those judges who are most 'creative' that garner the most accolades and that vie for recognition as 'great judges'. *See* Allan C. Hutchinson, *Laughing at the Gods: Great Judges and How they Made the Common Law* (2012).

[18] *Supra*, note 1 at 90.

nodding acquaintance with law and, in particular, lawyers' cautions against law acting as a bulwark of determinacy in a seething sea of ethical contestation.

For many, the distinguishing feature of good lawyering is the ability to make 'creative' interpretations: it is more prized as an enviable talent than stigmatized as an ethical failing. Admittedly, Wendel refers to '*excessively* creative and aggressive interpretations of legal norms'.[19] But the line between lawyers being moderately and excessively creative in their interpretive efforts is very fine and murky. Mindful of how much work this good faith duty to interpret is intended to do in the Wendelian scheme of things, it seems an unpromising basis on which to build a whole account of legal ethics. Good faith is too vague a notion to resolve detailed and subtle issues of ethical performance. Moreover, what would it mean to enforce this requirement against lawyers perceived as acting too unreasonably or unconscientiously?

Finally, there lingers within Wendel's justificatory account an assumption that law is something that stands outside the work and world of lawyering. Indeed, to act as a viable constraint on lawyers' conduct, law must be able to be depicted as a body of norms that stands as something that is sufficiently separate from lawyers. While there might be some modest defense of the idea that legislation is created and understood independently, it is much more difficult to sustain the claim that common law and constitutional doctrines are generated without the considerable input of lawyers. The fact is that a legal system has the laws that it has because of, not in spite of what lawyers do: the clients they represent, the causes they advocate and the strategies they deploy all influence the law's content and substance. So appreciated, it becomes much less reassuring to connect legal ethics' legitimacy to the establishment of legal entitlements when those entitlements are the function of the very conduct that they are supposed to regulate and channel. This seems a gaping and devastating shortcoming in Wendel's positivist-inspired account.

An instructive and revealing discussion of the 'good faith' requirement takes place around the issue of frivolity in pleadings. In a provision that is typical of many jurisdictions, Rule 11(b), (2) of the

[19] *Id.* at 117 (emphasis added).

U.S. Federal Rules of Civil Procedure obliges lawyers to certify that any legal claims made in their pleadings are, among other things, 'warranted by existing law or by a nonfrivolous argument for extending, modifying, or reversing existing law or for establishing new law... after an inquiry reasonable under the circumstances'.[20] While there is considerable agreement about the need to discipline lawyers who burden the courts and other litigants with unrealistic claims, it has been notoriously difficult to agree on what 'nonfrivolous' means. It has only been found where there is clear evidence that no reasonable attorney could have concluded that such a claim *might* be established and also that it was made for improper purposes; the individual lawyer's belief as to reasonableness of claim is key. As one civil proceduralist has noted, 'today's frivolity may be tomorrow's law, and the law often grows by an organic process in which a concept is conceived, then derided as absurd (and clearly not the law), then recognized as theoretically tenable (though not the law), then accepted as the law.'[21] Such an experience is hardly supportive of Wendel's willingness to place all his ethical eggs in the basket of the 'good faith' argument. While there is a strong case to be made for including a good faith constraint in any series of ethical injunctions, it is wildly optimistic to make it the almost exclusive benchmark by which to control and discipline lawyers.

THE INTERPRETIVE CHALLENGE

Wendel concedes that his whole justificatory enterprise 'stand[s] or fall[s] on the capacity of the law to yield moderately determinate meanings'. He is very alert to the claim that 'law may be so manipulable that an obligation of fidelity to law is inherently unworkable.' Nevertheless, he is equally adamant that there exists sufficient determinacy in law to underwrite his justificatory account of legal

[20] Until amended in 1993, 'nonfrivolous argument' used to read 'a good faith argument'. *See Nemeroff v. Abelson*, 620 F. 2d 339 (2d Cir. 1980) and *Kinee v. Abraham Lincoln Fed. Saving & Loan Assoc.*, 365 F. Supp. 975 (E.D.Pa. 1973).

[21] D. Michael Risinger, 'Honesty in Pleading and Its Enforcement: Some "Striking" Problems with Federal Rule of Civil Procedure', 11, 61 *Minn. L. Rev.* 1 at 57 (1976). For a more jurisprudence-oriented discussion, *see* Sanford Levinson, 'Frivolous Cases: Do Lawyers Really Know Anything at All'? 24 *Osgoode Hall L. J.* 353 (1987).

ethics. For him, there is a 'zone of reasonableness'. While 'people are likely to disagree in good faith about how to specify an abstract ethical value as a concrete maxim of action,' Wendel maintains that what lawyers know best is the law and so they should be expected to adhere to its imperatives, not morality's more diffuse injunctions. As such, legal interpretation is presented as a professional craft that contains its own standards of excellence and reasonableness. As he puts it, 'being an ethical lawyer means doing well at the craft of lawyering.'[22]

Although Wendel recognizes the importance of these jurisprudential matters to his 'fidelity to law' account of legal ethics, he does little more than make repetitive assertions of the existence of a 'zone of reasonableness'. He gives little sustained attention to how that might actually be achieved in a robust and reliable way. He says that the threshold of interpretive plausibility is not so low as a 'laugh test', but might be met 'if a lawyer would be comfortable in making the argument to a judge for whom she clerked, a professor she respects, or a colleague who is known for her good sense and judgment'. Taking his lead from the disputed ideas of Owen Fiss,[23] Wendel is satisfied to put his jurisprudential faith in the traditional resources and techniques of the legal community: 'if that reasoning passes muster, by the standards of the interpretive community, then the lawyer is justified in ethical terms.'[24]

Pitched at such a level of generality, this seems a tempting and viable solution. But, as crafted (and crafty) lawyers know, legal interpretation takes place in more specific and concrete circumstances.[25]

[22] *Supra*, note 1 at 176, 13, 53, 90 and 211.

[23] Owen Fiss, 'Objectivity and Interpretation', 34 *Stan. L. Rev.* 739 (1982). For critical responses, *see* Stanley Fish, *Doing What Comes Naturally: Change, Rhetoric, and the Practice of Theory in Literary and Legal Studies* (1990) and Allan C. Hutchinson, *Dwelling on the Threshold: Critical Essays on Modern Legal Thought* 125–82 (1988).

[24] *Supra*, note 1 at 53, 58 and 207.

[25] Of course, the debate over law's indeterminacy is the stuff of protracted jurisprudential disagreement. For my own extended account of legal interpretation as a playful performance in law's language game, *see* Game, *supra*, note 16 and *Evolution and the Common Law* (2005). While rules clearly exist, the precise meaning of those rules is always contingent and elusive in particular circumstances. No set of rules stands apart from interpretive attempts at its hermeneutical appropriation; there is no uncontentious interpretation that can claim to be

Indeed, in two of the main illustrative examples that Wendel relies on, his insistence that 'for any given area of law, there is a core area of agreement in interpretive judgments' begins to look more than a little shaky.[26] Insofar as agreement exists, it will be as much about the shared substantive values and commitments of lawyers as it will be about technical merits of the lawyers' interpretive craft.

Resorting to the traditional chestnut of the 'no vehicles in the park' hypothetical, Wendel argues that, while there is a penumbral area of uncertainty, there is a core of professional agreement that some situations fall squarely within the rule. He contends that 'if the statute means anything, it means that you cannot drive a souped-up sports car through the park.'[27] Yet, as most lawyers would agree, that conclusion can become much less obvious or incontestable in particular circumstances: What if there was a sports car exhibition being held in the park? What if the sports car was being used as a makeshift ambulance? By positing these hypotheticals, I am not asserting that the rule is meaningless or that there are not instances of determinacy. I am simply arguing that there is no uncontroversial, fixed or plain meaning that can be referenced outside of any particular contingent context or joined debate of legal interpretation.[28] And, without such an available and sanctioned core of meaning, Wendel's jurisprudential claims are in trouble as a persuasive foundation for his neo-traditional version of legal ethics.

The same problem arises in the more telling and troubling situation of the Torture Memos. Wendel wants to condemn John Yoo's advice as indefensible and argue that it does not pass muster as legal advice at all: 'waterboarding is the souped-up sport car of

the authoritative measure against which other interpretations can be contrasted. As such, determinacy and indeterminacy are not pre-interpretive features of the law, but the resulting products of legal interpretation. *See, for example*, Duncan Kennedy, 'Thoughts on Coherence, Social Values and National Tradition in Private Law', in Martijn Hesselink, ed., *The Politics of a European Civil Code* 9 (2006); Duncan Kennedy, 'A Left Phenomenological Alternative to the Hart/Kelsen Theory of Legal Interpretation', in D. Kennedy, ed., *Legal Reasoning: Collected Essays* 154 (2009).

26 *Supra*, note 1 at 22.

27 *Id.* at 15.

28 For my own extended take on 'vehicles in the park', *see* Hutchinson, 'In the Park: A Jurisprudential Primer', 48 *Osgoode Hall L.J.* 337 (2010).

the prohibitions on torture.' He leaves no room for doubt that 'the objection… is not so much that it is bad moral advice; rather, it is that it is bad legal advice – the law simply does not permit what interrogators at Guantanamo Bay… have done to detainees.' Yet, as much as he may wish it so, his laudable moral sensibilities do not warrant that 'there really is not any disagreement, in good faith, about the meaning and application of [waterboarding as torture].'[29] The problem is that, as long as Yoo, the memo writer, believed that he was acting in good faith in arriving at a reading of the law requested by his presidential client, then Wendel's dismissal of the legal opinion is much less convincing. Indeed, as Yoo himself said in a subsequent hearing before a House panel, 'there is certainly room for disagreement among reasonable people, acting in good faith, on these questions, but I still believe we gave the best answers we could on the basis of the legal matters available to us.'[30]

For all his declamations (and most lawyers' desire to condemn Yoo as not only a moral scoundrel, but as a grossly incompetent lawyer), Wendel is simply unable to be as categorical as he would wish and, more important, needs to be in establishing the operational efficacy of his moral injunction to show 'fidelity to law'. This is symptomatic of the more general failing of his interpretive claims. Wendel has little to say to lawyers or anyone else in those circumstances where we most need advice – when lawyers disagree about what the law is. It is hardly a recommendation for his account of legal ethics that it only works when there is a widely shared or relatively unchallenged agreement on particular aspects of lawyerly conduct or legal interpretation. The real test of any proposed ethical stance is whether it offers any assistance or guidance in those so-called hard cases where there is professional disagreement or contestation. And when you add to that the difficulties of pinning

[29] *Supra*, note 1 at 15, 181 and 182.

[30] *Washington Post*, Friday, June 27, 2008. *See* John Yoo, *Crisis and Command: A History of Executive Power from George Washington to George W. Bush* (2010). *See also* Dawn E. Johnsen, 'Faithfully Executing the Laws: Internal Legal Constraints on Executive Power' (2007) 54 *Ucla L. Rev.* 1559 and Kathleen Clark, 'Ethical Issues Raised by the OLC Torture Memorandum' (2005) 1 *Journal of National Security Law & Policy* 455 at 458–63.

down the constraining moral force of good faith interpretation, Wendel's reliance on 'fidelity to law' looks even more problematic.

WENDELIAN WOBBLES

The bottom line is that Wendel has very little to tell lawyers about what they might do or how they might think about what they might do when they are confronted with the familiar ethical dilemmas of professional legal practice. When the going gets tough, Wendel has nothing to say other than 'show fidelity to law.' He concedes that 'there is nothing wrong with having a moral dialogue with clients about whether to exercise the client's legal entitlements.' But, apart from the fact that it is unclear what the Wendelian lawyer would say *qua* lawyer in such a dialogue, such concessions are unhelpful if moral considerations are simply not part of the lawyer's discursive universe: 'lawyers, when they act in a professional capacity, should be concerned only with the legal justice of the clients' situation.'[31] Two of Wendel's examples point to the moral vacuity of his general account of legal ethics.

The first situation is straightforward. B(orrower) is in financial straits and loans $5,000 by way of a promissory note from his wealthy neighbor, L(ender). L lets the note lapse. A number of years later, their financial situations are reversed and L feels obliged to seek the money back from B. For no apparent reason, B directs his lawyer to defend an action by L. The central question is whether B's lawyer should plead a solid limitation defense against the claim. Wendel argues that, whatever the moral failing of the client, the lawyer not only can, but also should plead the limitations defense on behalf of B. 'Regardless of any moral qualms the lawyer may have', he maintains, 'the ethics of lawyers acting in a professional capacity is different from the ethics of ordinary people.'[32] While the recognition of the differences in roles is well taken, the basis for the precise distinction in this instance remains undeveloped.

In this scenario, there is considerable disagreement about what the lawyer should do and why; it is a classic problem that tends to

[31] *Supra*, note 1 at 135 and 11.

[32] *Id.* at 28 and 29.

divide many lawyers and ethicists.[33] Wendel's only advice to the lawyer is to comply, dissuade the client from proceeding or withdraw. But there is no discursive framework or set of resources that Wendel offers through which the lawyer might be able to determine what to do. He is unable to say much by way of ethical advice other than that withdrawal should be 'a last resort'.[34] While there is no easy or obvious answer to this professional quandary (and it would be silly to expect one), the worth of any ethical account is its ability to inform debate and structure available arguments. Wendel's account has little to contribute in identifying a more informative set of questions to be asked, the conversational resources available to address them and the possible answers to be offered. By reducing ethics to 'fidelity to law', he rejects its characterization and resolution as matters of professional concern.

The second example is *Spaulding v. Zimmerman*.[35] Z's lawyer obtains a medical report on S that shows that S has an immediately life-threatening aneurism as a result of a car accident in which Z is at fault; S's own doctor has missed this in his medical examination. Although the report is confidential, Z's lawyer has a duty to hand over the medical report, if asked by S's lawyer: no such request is forthcoming. Can or should Z's lawyer voluntarily give the medical report to S's lawyer? If he does not, S will not be able to have the necessary life-saving surgery and might die. But, if he does, S's damages claim against his client Z will increase substantially. Almost all commentators, including Wendel, agree that Z's lawyers should have at least consulted with his client about whether to preserve confidentiality or disclose. But there is sharp debate over what Z's lawyer should have done if Z insisted on keeping it confidential.[36]

Wendel's response is revealing. Noting that this is a hard case in that the parties' legal entitlements – confidentiality on one side and

[33] *See, for example*, Stephen Pepper, 'Lawyers' Ethics in the Gap Between Law and Justice', 40 *S. Texas L. Rev.* 181 at 189–90 (1999) and Thomas Shaffer, 'The Legal Ethics of Radical Individualism', 65 *Texas L. Rev.* 963 at 977–9 (1987).

[34] *Supra*, note 1 at 128.

[35] 116 N.W. 2nd 704 (Minnesota, 1962).

[36] *See, for example*, Roger Cramton and Lori Knowles, 'Professional Secrecy and Its Exceptions: Spaulding v. Zimmerman Revisited', 83 *Minn. L. Rev.* 63 (1998).

the right to the document on the other – are evenly balanced, he concludes that:

> For my own part, I find the possibility of non-disclosure intolerable for moral reasons, but if Zimmerman refuses to give informed consent to disclosure, the best course of action would be for his lawyer to disclose anyway and run the risk of professional discipline. A ... suspension ... would be a serious harm to Zimmerman's lawyer, but it is one that he may be morally obligated to incur in order to avoid harm to Spaulding.[37]

This response is baffling; it runs contrary to the whole thrust of Wendel's approach to legal ethics. It may well be true and noble that he considers that the option of nondisclosure is personally 'intolerable' for him, but he is unforthcoming about those reasons. Moreover, this personal response is hardly the basis for a decision to withdraw as Z's lawyer, let alone a general piece of advice to other lawyers to follow suit. The main point of his account of legal ethics is supposed to be that the ethical duty of lawyers is to 'subordinate' or 'exclude' ordinary moral concerns from their professional lives and 'as long as the lawyer acts within the law, her actions may not be evaluated in ordinary moral terms.' Therefore, it would seem to follow that Wendelian lawyers not only can, but should and perhaps must respect their clients' legal entitlement not to disclose and can do so without 'moral qualms'; this is consistent with his stance on Borrower's instructions.[38]

If that is the case, it is hard to see on what basis Wendel is placing his own personal moral commitments above his professional lawyering duty in advising others to withdraw as a matter of 'moral obligation'. Again, Wendel offers no explanation of why this would be the case or even how we might go about reaching or not reaching such a decision. As these two applications display, Wendel's 'fidelity to law' model is less a theory of legal ethics than a jurisprudential account of why there is little need for one. On his justificatory account, legal ethics is a casualty of the adherence to an uncompromising (and wrong-headed) positivism that squeezes morality from both the nature of law and the nature of lawyering. Within Wendel's stripped-down account, lawyers' professional ethics require

[37] *Supra*, note 1 at 75.
[38] *Id.* at 155, 157, 29 and 86.

that lawyers do little more than vigorously pursue their clients' ends within the bounds of the law: the only ethical constraint in play is the inadequately thin and minimalist one of 'respecting the law'.

Viewed through his proposed justificatory account of legal ethics, Wendel's conclusion that 'in the end, being an ethical lawyer means doing well at the craft of lawyering' is a celebration of neither the ethical lawyer nor the elusive craft of lawyering.[39] There is much more to being an ethical lawyer than being adept at the craft of lawyering. What we do with those crafted skills and for whom – is there really no difference between constructing torture racks or hospital beds? – is surely part of the ethical debate that lawyers must have if they are to deserve the label 'ethical'. For legal ethicists of a Wendelian persuasion, legal ethics becomes little more than so much unnecessary philosophical baggage on the otherwise prosaic journey to professional competence.

CONCLUSION

I have been hard on Wendel (and, by extension, all his traditionalist colleagues) for the failure to offer an adequate account of legal ethics that is worthy of the name. My main bone of contention is not that I necessarily disagree with any particular course of action that he might recommend in particular situations. It is that Wendel offers lawyers no genuine ethical guidance about what counts as moral sensitivity, moral judgment and moral conviction and how they might incorporate such qualities into the ethical hurly-burly of their daily professional lives. Telling other lawyers what you personally might do (as both lawyer and commentator) in any particular situation does not amount to a theory of legal ethics. That theoretical task would require laying out a more subtle and sophisticated set of arguments and reasons that could be accessed and utilized by lawyers in identifying and reaching solutions to intractable ethical challenges. This is no small or simple task, but it is one that must be undertaken.[40]

[39] *Id.* at 211.

[40] Important efforts at this reconstructive task have already been made. *See* William Simon, *The Practice of Justice: A Theory of Lawyers' Ethics* (1998) and David Luban, *Legal Ethics and Human Dignity* (2007).

4

The Standard Model

As I have sought to emphasize, if lawyers want to receive more professional respect for their work, they will have to earn it by reframing their ethical duties and taking them more seriously. This will not be done, as the neo-traditionalists seem to recommend, by offering better explanations and novel justifications for existing practices. Instead, it will require a genuine willingness to change what lawyers do and, as important, how lawyers think about what they do. A preparatory step to this essential task is to scrutinize more thoroughly the structure and failings of the Standard Conception of legal ethics and professional responsibility.

CLEARING THE GROUND

A revised theory of legal ethics will need to reclaim and rethink the nature of this public-spiritedness that is supposed to animate professional practice if lawyers are to retain the privileges and independence they presently claim. The argument that there is a strongly differentiated role morality that lawyers are to interpose between their personal and their professional lives can only be justified if it serves the public interest more than it does their own self-interest. In short, it is incumbent on the profession to ensure that the interests of justice are placed squarely and regularly at the forefront of professional concerns. As such, the primary justificatory challenge is to interrogate the dominant model of the ethical lawyer that informs the practicing lives of lawyers. In particular, it will be necessary to develop a more sophisticated vocabulary and fuller set of discursive resources that will be up to the task of negotiating better the difficult ethical terrain of professional lawyering: On whose behalf should legal services be deployed? And how should lawyers operate in the service of those clients and causes?

However, as a preliminary matter, it is necessary to clear away some of the conceptual debris that presently hinders efforts to move forward. First, the place to begin any reconstructive project is with the Standard Conception of ethical lawyering and its institutional privileging of client partisanship, substantive neutrality and professional non-accountability. Rather than grant it a presumptive ethical authority and unassailable institutional status as Wendel does, it is necessary to subject it to a more searching and unconditional critique. While the Standard Conception has obvious and cogent appeal in the criminal law context, there are no compelling or consistent reasons to extend this rationale to the noncriminal context; the institutional dynamics and moral considerations of criminal and noncriminal practice are very different. This does not mean that some components of the Standard Conception (e.g., confidentiality, conflict of interests, etc.) are not worth keeping, albeit in a possibly revised form. But there will be little progress made if the Standard Conception is considered the default paradigm for defining and evaluating professional responsibility. A richer and more nuanced theory and practice of legal ethics will want to put topics, such as client selection, litigation strategy, negotiation tactics and the like, back on the agenda of debate and development.

Second, it is imperative that legal ethicists, like Wendel, abandon their attempts to annex traditional legal ethics to a positivist account of law. Even within the positivist canon, there is no justification for treating the law's morality or substantive justice as something that is outside the lawyers' frame of reference or legitimate concern. Although positivists can be distinguished by their insistence that the domains of law and morality must be kept separate in the conceptual effort to fix and identify the necessary terms of law's nature and validity, they still recommend that there are many other ways law and morality can and should interact. Indeed, leading positivists are at pains to explain how positivism does not demand that lawyers pay no attention to law's moral content or substantive worth; much of their work is devoted to addressing the moral failings of extant law.[1] Consequently, it does not follow at all that Wendel's commitment to a positivist understanding of law should or can lead to an account of professional ethics that eschews resort to the moral merit of law's substance and the ethical quality of its practitioners' actions. To advocate for such a hands-off and agnostic stance, as Wendel does, is a perversion of positivism, not a defensible corollary of it.

Third, if lawyers are to be properly treated as 'public actors' as Wendel and his traditionalist colleagues intimate,[2] then it is essential that there is a more informed and fuller appreciation of what public goals and communal interests lawyers are serving in their professional practice under the Standard Conception. Without more, there is no justification for why the 'public interest' should be thought to be exhausted or fulfilled by lawyers simply devoting themselves to the facilitation and advancement of their clients' private interests. It is the element of public-spiritedness that sets lawyers apart from other tradespersons and that warrants their considerable privileges and powers.[3] The moral obligations of lawyers as self-regulating professionals, therefore, extend beyond exclusive concern with furthering their clients' interests. Instead, they should be expected, not simply encouraged, to include the public interest in any serious remapping of their ethical obligations and professional performance. The fact that what counts as the public interest will

[1] John Gardner, 'Legal Positivism: 5½ Myths', 46 *Am. J. of Juris.* 199 at 213 (2000). *See also*, H. L. A. Hart, 'Legal Positivism', in *Encyclopaedia of Philosophy IV*, 418 (1967); Jules Coleman and Brian Leiter, 'Legal Positivism', in *A Companion to Philosophy of Law and Legal Theory* (D. Patterson ed., 1996); Leslie Green, 'Legal Positivism', in *Stanford Encyclopedia of Philosophy* http://plato.stanford.edu/entries/legal-positivism/; M. Kramer, *In Defence of Legal Positivism* 1 (1999); and Andrei Marmor, 'Legal Positivism: Still Descriptive and Morally Neutral', 26 *Oxf. J. of Legal Studies* 683 (2006). There are, of course, less positivistic accounts of law that insist that morality is at the heart of the legal enterprise, including the jurisprudential identification of law's defining nature. *See* Lon L. Fuller, *The Morality of Law* (rev. ed. 1965) and, also, Ronald Dworkin, *Law's Empire* (1986).

[2] W. Bradley Wendel, *Lawyers and Fidelity to Law* 13 (2010).

[3] *See* R. Pound, *The Lawyer from Antiquity to Modern Times: With Particular Reference to the Development of Bar Associations in the United States* (1953); T. Parsons, 'A Sociologist Looks at the Legal Profession', in T. Parsons, *Essays in Sociological Theory* (1958); and Deborah Rhode, 'The Professionalism Problem', 39 *W. & M. L. Rev.* 283 (1998).

always be contested and contingent is more appropriately treated as a warning, not a negation of its importance.

THE TRADITIONAL ROLE

The dominant model of the ethical lawyer is centered almost entirely on a very inward-looking view of the lawyer-client relationship. The clients are perceived as autonomous in determining their own best interests; it is assumed that no one knows in the final analysis what is in the clients' own best interests other than the clients themselves. For their part, lawyers are expected to advance those interests with unconditional vigor, unquestioning loyalty, genuine candor and marked partisanship. In the language of the U.S. professional rules, the basic thrust of ethical lawyering is to encompass 'the lawyer's obligation zealously to protect and pursue a client's legitimate interests, within the bounds of the law'.[4] It is very much as secondary players, not primary actors, that lawyers are supposed to function and find legitimation for their ethical standing.

Under this model, the legal professional fulfills a largely technical or service role: lawyers possess a special set of talents and techniques that they deploy strategically for the advantage of the people who hire them. While almost indifferent to (and proudly so) the identity of their clients, lawyers think of themselves as more chosen than choosing. However, once hired, lawyers are required to put their clients' interests ahead of all others, including the lawyers' own interests, provided that their clients' goals are not legally impermissible. As such, ethical lawyers are portrayed as super-technocrats who serve the legal system best and fulfill its broader goals of justice when they judge neither the moral worthiness of their clients nor the social justness of their causes.[5] Lawyers might say, along with Tennyson, that, like the Light Brigade, 'theirs not to make reply,/ Theirs not to reason why,/ Theirs but to do and die.'[6]

[4] *Model Rules of Prof'l Conduct* pmbl. para. 9 (2002).

[5] For a sophisticated account of this traditional role, *see* Sharon Dolovich, 'Ethical Lawyering and the Possibility of Integrity', 70 *Fordham L. Rev.* 1629 (2002); William Simon, *The Practice of Justice* 12 (1998); Trevor Farrow, 'Sustainable Professionalism', 46 *Osgoode Hall L.J.* 51 (2008).

[6] Alfred, Lord Tennyson, '*The Charge of the Light Brigade*' (1854).

As part and parcel of this professional compact, lawyers are empowered to engage in behavior that might otherwise be considered inappropriate and even unethical in a nonprofessional setting. Except in the most egregious circumstances, lawyers are expected to be single-minded in their devotion to their clients' causes and to use whatever legal means are at their disposal to advance those causes. This means that lawyers are entitled (and, sometimes, required) to become 'masters of manipulation' in that they massage rules, distinctions, meanings and facts to serve their clients' purposes.[7] Indeed, the ability to dissemble and quibble in the most creative and crafted way possible is often considered the hallmark of gifted lawyers. At its most extreme, this facility for manipulation can be tantamount to allowing lawyers to lie (e.g., asserting false statements) and cheat (e.g., advancing unreasonable and unverifiable claims and defenses) on behalf of their clients. Indeed, some contend that such actions may well be encouraged and excused in pressing circumstances; personal vices might well be tolerated as professional virtues. The question for the law's zealous advocate is less about whether to lie or cheat, but what are the limits to the professional kind of lies or cheating that are permitted.

Of course, the language of 'zealous advocacy' is stark and uncompromising. It suggests a certain irrational fervor in that lawyers are supposed to commit themselves to advancing their clients' interests in an excessive way that smacks of partisan fanaticism. As a basis for ethical justification, this seems a dubious platform on which to build an attractive model of professional responsibility. While such servitude and loyalty may be appropriate for dogs or religious fanatics, it hardly promises a balanced approach to life or lawyering. Indeed, the imagery of 'zealotry' shares a little with the kind of unthinking and unhinged dedication that motivates terrorists and other reviled figures. Moreover, such zealots at least can make the claim that they are genuinely, if perversely, committed to a cause or ideal. Lawyers have no such response; they act only out of professional obligation, not personal belief. As Lord Eldon neatly put it,

[7] Richard A. Matasar, 'The Pain of Moral Lawyering', 75 *Iowa L. Rev.* 975, 975–6 (1990). *See also* Daniel Markovits, *A Modern Legal Ethics* (2008); and Monroe H. Freedman, *Lawyers' Ethics in an Adversary System* 9–24 (1975).

the lawyer lends 'his exertions to all; himself to none'.[8] If such a practice of lawyering is to be defended as an authentic and proud ethical ideal, it demands a very rigorous and powerful justification. 'Zealotry' simply does not cut it.

Although this traditional depiction of lawyers' professional role recommends that lawyers take an amoral or a conscience-off stance in fulfilling their professional duties, it does so based on a very particular political justification of lawyers' appropriate social role. Indeed, to appreciate this apparently constrained vision of ethical lawyering, it is necessary to reference the deeper political and ethical theory on which it is based. In such a broader light, the traditional account of a strongly differentiated role between personal and professional ethical commitments is much more understandable, even if it remains far from compelling or justifiable. The underpinnings are borrowed directly from liberal political and legal theory.

In negotiating the relations between government and individual citizens, the legal profession is considered to have an important role to play. Apart from holding regular elections and respecting various other institutional devices of accountability, government must abide by the legal rules in force as part of the overall commitment to the Rule of Law. Moreover, individual citizens are entitled to rely on the full range of legal rights and entitlements in their dealings with the government and each other. Because there is an imbalance of power between government and individuals (particularly when the law becomes increasingly complex), the legal profession operates as a necessary bulwark against the oppressive exercise of official power. Because it fulfills this vital role, it is essential that the legal profession does not put its own professional interests or social agenda ahead of those of the people it is intended to serve. To do so would compromise both the Rule of Law and liberal democratic theory.

Accordingly, the legal profession is required to regard itself as neutral on the substance and form of the law. Their commitment is to the legal system that, even when lawyers are working around and within it, must be accepted as given. In their professional lives,

[8] *Ex Parte Lloyd* Mont. 70n (1822). For a modern defense of this stance, *see* Tim Dare, *The Counsel of Rogues?* (2009).

ethical lawyers serve the legal process and, therefore, society at large by ensuring that people can access and activate their legal rights. Within such a justificatory framework, it would be unjust and indefensible if lawyers did more or less than that. They best fulfill the political demands of their professional roles by remaining ethically neutral in regard to both the clients they serve and the methods they deploy. Not only is there no need for lawyers to act in solidarity with their clients' stances, but also there are important political and moral reasons lawyers should be consciously indifferent to their clients' causes and goals.

The origins and justification of this lawyering image are very much tied in with the operation of the criminal trial process. Indeed, if there is any ethically compelling purchase for this model, it is to be found in the role of criminal defense counsel.[9] Since Queen Caroline's prosecution in the early nineteenth century, it has been accepted that an advocate must do all that he can to 'save that client by all means and expedients' and 'must not regard the alarm, the torments, the destruction which he may bring upon others'.[10] As accused individuals, citizens are pitted against the state, with all its resources and power, and are often in urgent need of a reliable and informed friend who is always and unconditionally on their side. Charged with the task of raising a reasonable doubt, criminal lawyers are expected to commit themselves to doing all they can to ensure that their clients are acquitted and that the state does not exercise its punitive powers without respecting the rights of those it proceeds against; this applies whether accused persons are guilty or innocent. By so doing, advocates will ensure that they act in the most deserving and honorable way possible. It will be entirely beside the point what the lawyer thinks about the guilt or innocence of the client; the lawyer is supposed to make a sharp distinction between her own personal views and the performance

[9] *See* David Layton, 'The Criminal Defense Lawyer's Role', 27 *Dalhousie. L.J.* 379 (2004).

[10] 2 *Trial of Queen Caroline* 8 (J. Nightingale ed., 1821). Apparently, Chief Justice Cockburn told Lord Brougham, at a dinner party some time after his speech, that while it was appropriate to be a zealous advocate, a lawyer ought not to be an 'assassin'. *See also* David M. Tanovich, 'Law's Ambition and the Reconstruction of Role Morality in Canada', 28 *Dalhousie L.J.* 267, 271 (2005).

of her professional role. Although this might lead to some substantive injustices in particular circumstances (i.e., guilty persons will be acquitted), it will serve society best in the long run and over the largest number of cases.

Of course, not all or even most lawyering is concerned with the criminal justice system. However, the criminal defense model holds great theoretical sway in defining the basis and limits of lawyers' ethical role generally. The strict adversarial ethic has been largely transposed to the noncriminal law setting so that private lawyers are expected to adhere to a similar partisan role in representing their clients. Within such an account of lawyers in a democratic society, it will be apparent that lawyers are thought to advance the public interest by standing squarely in the citizens' corner and promoting or protecting their private interests against the government or against other citizens, in accordance with existing law and policy. As such, although this professional role is decidedly amoral, in that lawyers are not expected or required to take up their clients' interests and causes as their own or to defend them morally, it does have a putative moral and democratic underpinning. The legal profession is at its most institutionally moral when it adopts an amoral stance toward legal practice.

HIRED GUNS

Many terms and images have been employed to designate this dominant model of the ethical lawyer – hired hand, amoral technician, special friend and the like. The most colorful and, I would suggest, most instructive is that of the 'hired gun'. Drawing on the medieval practice of 'trial by battle' and appointed champions,[11] the term 'hired gun' regained currency in North America in the 1960s. It invoked the fabled image of the Western gunfighter – a man-in-black who sold his superior talents with a gun to those who needed or could afford his firepower. Of course, although these figures worked on the margins of law and the establishment, this did not

[11] *See* Joseph C. France, 'The American Judicial System – The Lawyers', 35th *Conference Ann. Rep. A.B.A.* 411, 413 (1912); Henry S. Drinker, *Legal Ethics* 12–14 (1953); M. J. Russell, 'Hired Champions', 3 *Am. J. Legal Hist.* 242 (1959).

mean that they were bad by personal nature or professional undertaking: some found themselves on the side of justice, whereas others functioned more in the shadows. The gunslinger was true to his professional mission rather than that of his different clients and the varied causes they pursued.[12]

While obviously a caricature, it does fit nicely within the more traditional role of ethical lawyering. It draws on the depiction of legal work, especially litigation, as part of social warfare in which people are pitted against each other for social supremacy in a state-controlled arena. Although it invokes an imagery that is hardly flattering to the legal profession (or society at large), it does convey something of the popular perception that many lawyers do sell themselves to the highest bidder without regard to the justness of the clients' causes or motivations. Moreover, it captures the idea that lawyers are more than willing to do people's dirty work for them. The fact that they find themselves representing people with worthy ambitions and just causes is more by good fortune than deliberate design: they fulfill their highest professional and ethical mandate by remaining neutral on matters of substance and justice.

In romanticizing the hard-headed and unsentimental dimensions of the legal role, the character of the hired gun is of dubious provenance and raises more difficulties than it resolves. Indeed, the hired gun metaphor, even if dressed in more attractive rhetorical garb, should be deeply troubling to lawyers. While hired guns or even assassins are not necessarily without honor or scruples,[13] the treatment of lawyers as hired guns does more to compromise the ethical

[12] Monroe Freedman, 'The Lawyer as Hired Gun', 62 *N.Y. St. B.J.* 48 (1990); Joseph Allegretti, 'Have Briefcase Will Travel: An Essay on the Lawyer as Hired Gun', 24 *Creighton L. Rev.* 747 (1990); Robert P. Lawry, 'The Central Moral Tradition of Lawyering', 19 *Hofstra L. Rev.* 311 (1990); Ted Schneyer, 'Some Sympathy for the Hired Gun', 41 *J. Legal Educ.* 11 at 11 (1991); Paul Haskell, *Why Lawyers Behave as They Do* 85–92 (1998); Michael Krauss, 'The Lawyer as Limo: A Brief History of the Hired Gun', 8 *U. Chi. L. Sch. Roundtable* 325 (2001).

[13] As the assassin Sparafucile in Verdi's *Rigoletto* puts it when asked to renege on a deal with the Duke to murder someone by killing the Duke himself, 'What the devil do you mean? Am I a thief? Am I a bandit? What client of mine has ever been cheated? This man pays me, and I shall deliver.' *See* Giuseppe Verdi, *Rigoletto* act 3, sc. 13. For a more modern defense, *see* Haskell, *supra* note 12; and Christine Parker & Adrian Evans, *Inside Lawyers' Ethics* (2007).

virtues of lawyers than complement them. Any effort to defend the image of the hired gun as an accurate and even desirable characterization of the lawyer's role should be disquieting. Nevertheless, while it may well exaggerate the strongly differentiated role of lawyers, it does point up some of the less palatable features of the legal professional. Of course, critics have heavily pilloried this traditional role or Standard Conception. For the most part, this is entirely warranted. Some of the more obvious limitations and drawbacks of this 'hired gun' model include:

- **Outside of Criminal Law** – Whatever traction the traditional model has in the criminal context, it has little in civil litigation. The basic thrust of its relevance for the criminal context is based on the government's power and its enormous potential for abusive and overbearing conduct. It is important that individual accused be able to have someone in their corner who is single-mindedly devoted to their interests; defense lawyers satisfy a clear public interest by keeping the government in check and obliging it to prove its cases by lawful and fair means. In the noncriminal context, this dynamic is conspicuous by its absence. Indeed, it may well be that one private party is utilizing the legal process and his or her access to legal services to oppress another private actor.
- **Beyond Adversarialism** – If the traditional model has little applicability to the litigation process, it has even less in non-adversarial settings. Lawyers are asked to play diverse and heterogeneous roles in modern legal practice. Much lawyering is transactional and non-adversarial in nature (e.g., drafting wills and incorporating organizations). Indeed, in line with moves toward more consensual modes of dispute resolution, the guiding image of the hired gun is particularly ill-matched to the ostensibly cooperative activities of negotiation, mediation and the like. Such a stance seems more likely to impede and even sabotage the successful and productive resolution of a dispute.
- **Three's a Crowd** – Many legal interactions involve multiple parties and are rarely reducible to the simple binary, zero-sum or black-and-white logic that seems implicit in the hired gun scenario. In its most uncompromising application, the hired gun ideal recommends that lawyers must 'treat outsiders as if they were

barbarians and enemies'.[14] This is a very crude and objectionable dynamic that does no justice to lawyers or the legal system; it ignores the underlying public dimension and justification for the hired gun. Although lawyers might well be required to put the welfare of their clients ahead of others and their own, it does not mean that they cannot or should not take other interests into account and avoid doing them harm.

- **A Mismatch** – In order to work with some degree of efficacy and fairness, the traditional model must assume a basic equality between the parties in terms of the resources that they have at their disposal. This is rarely the case and is often quite the opposite; one party is often overmatched by the other. As the cost of lawyers becomes ever further beyond the pocket of many individuals, the mismatch between parties can seriously and substantially affect the outcome of legal proceedings or dealings. Like in the more general market, the disparities of wealth and resources will undermine fairness in the legal conflict between the haves and the have-nots; this is especially the case in disputes between individuals and corporations. As such, the hired gun image exacerbates rather than works to overcome the injustices that result from social inequalities.[15]
- **Shirking Responsibility** – The traditional model allows lawyers to absolve themselves of most responsibility for the actual legal outcomes that occur in their cases. Any substantive injustice that might happen is said to be the fault of the legal rules in effect and/or the actions of judges and juries. Yet the hired gun image fails to acknowledge the pivotal role that lawyers play in shaping those legal rules in effect and the decisions reached by judges and juries. To a large extent, the existing legal rules and decisions reached are made because of, not in spite of, lawyers' efforts and arguments. Consequently, the cases that lawyers take and the arguments that they make influence the creation of legal rules and the pattern of decisions generated by them.

[14] Charles Curtis, 'The Ethics of Advocacy', 4 *Stan. L. Rev.* 3, 5 (1951). For an entirely different take, *see* Carrie Menkel-Meadow, 'Non-Adversarial Lawyering', 27 *Fla. St. U. L. Rev.* 153 (1999).

[15] Deborah L. Rhode, Symposium, 'Ethical Perspectives on Legal Practice', 37 *Stan. L. Rev.* 589 at 639–40 (1985).

- **Business as Usual** – The hired gun imagery operates as a shield for lawyers' unprofessional behavior. It allows them to masquerade their most favorable business practices as compatible with the specious amorality of a rigorous professionalism. Commerce has infiltrated legal practice under the guise of professionalism. Although originally offered as a corollary to the need to protect individual citizens' interests against government oppression, the traditional model of lawyering is being deployed to protect vested and corporate interests by helping to insulate them against popular accountability.[16] Accordingly, the 'public interest' has lost much of its critical bite and has been too easily interpreted to coincide with advancing the private interests of the legal profession and lawyers' clients.
- **An Empty Core** – The traditional model offers little advice or direction about how to choose between different means and courses of action; it seems entirely ends-driven. There are no real ethical constraints on lawyers' actions other than those to act within the law. It seems to equate being ethical with simply not being illegal. As such, this is an ethic shaved so thin as to be almost nonexistent. In particular, the hired gun ideal glosses over the crucial question of whether lawyers must do all that the law allows. There is no real guidance as to whether they are entitled to refrain from certain professional modes of legal behavior that are legal, but that are recommended against by other ethical imperatives (e.g., harm to third parties). As such, it fails to accomplish the basic requirements of a serious ethical framework.[17]
- **Less than Public** – The profession has managed to convince society (and, as important, itself) that its commitment to the 'public interest' can best be met by its adherence to such an undemanding model of ethical conduct. In short, the public interest has been given an attenuated and skewed meaning that tends to serve the business interests of the profession and powerful private

[16] Geoffrey C. Hazard Jr., 'The Future of Legal Ethics', 100 *Yale L.J.* 1239, 1245 (1990–1).

[17] Rob Atkinson, 'How the Butler Was Made to Do It: The Perverted Professionalism of the Remains of the Day', 105 *Yale L.J.* 177, 184 (1995). On the requirements of a sufficient ethical framework, *see supra* pp. 8–10.

interests more than interests of society at large in justice. The legal profession can go about its business not only without any critical regard to the clients it cultivates and the causes it serves, but also safe in the knowledge that this morally neutral stance fulfills the highest ethical goals of the profession and allows it to act as robustly as it can to serve its clients' interests and causes. In short, the profession's commitment to the 'public interest' can and does stand as a convenient legitimating cover for advancing the self-interest of the profession as well as those private interests most able to afford its service.

ADVERSARIAL POSSIBILITIES

These criticisms of the traditional or standard conception are telling. Taken together, they amount to a formidable indictment of the prevailing traditional approach to legal ethics and professionalism. Indeed, little about the traditional understanding of lawyers' professional role recommends it or warrants its continued priority as the dominant focus of the legal ethos. The question then is whether the traditional image of the ethical lawyer is so perverted and irredeemable that it must be abandoned in its entirety. To put it more pointedly, it must be asked whether that image can be salvaged by an act of imaginative reconstruction so that it is better able to meet the demands that the modern and varied conditions of legal practice place upon it. There is much to be said for junking the hired gun imagery entirely and forthwith; it does so much more harm than good that efforts to rescue it might well be throwing good money after bad. However, that possibility seems remote and unrealistic.

Many remain who are prepared to offer an affirmative defense of the traditional model, and a few more are willing to tolerate it. Nevertheless, there is a smaller group intent on crafting a more plausible, more satisfying and more persuasive model that can better guide and validate legal professional behavior as an ethical enterprise. Indeed, it would take little imagination to construct and develop a more attractive model of ethical lawyering that did not rely on or invoke the dubious imagery of the 'zealous advocate' or the 'hired hand'. The new models on offer are attractive and engaging. While they might not persuade the legal profession to make changes in its approach and acts, these reformulations offer a set of imperatives and parameters that can lay more direct claim to ethical legitimacy than the traditional imagery of zealous advocates or hired guns.[18]

However, this reformative work is not without serious problems. As with any effort at reframing and redirecting professional work, the most serious (and often neglected) challenge is to specify which parts of the prevailing institutional structure of law and society are to be treated as incapable of change (at least from a short- and mid-term perspective) and those that are not. It is relatively easy to propose a new theory of legal ethics when no institutional or social constraints are in play; the canvas is open and expansive. But it is entirely another thing to do so when there are real and persisting limits within which the work of refurbishment must take place. I maintain that this difficult and fraught project is what needs to be undertaken and accomplished. What it might lose in outright creativity, it might gain in practical relevance.

As things stand, the basic mandate for lawyers under the professional rules is to 'zealously assert[] the client's position *under the rules of the adversary system*'.[19] It is the proviso 'under the rules of the adversary system' that must be interrogated. So much about the adversary system is open to criticism and condemnation – it aggravates rather than abates social tension; it interferes with rather than enhances the search for truth; it exacerbates rather than ameliorates the inequalities between the parties; and so on. Most important, it gives rise to and helps validate the continuing authority of the hired gun imagery.[20] The adversary system is an institutional context that frames the work of lawyers as well as informs their professional self-image. As one commentator has noted, while 'the quality of the "hired gun" is close to the heart and substance of the litigating lawyer's role, ... the struggle to

[18] *See* Simon, *supra* note 5; Farrow, *supra* note 5; and Tanovich, *supra* note 10.

[19] *Model Rules of Prof'l Conduct* pmbl., para. 2 (2002) (emphasis added).

[20] The most convincing critique remains that of Neil Brooks. *See* Neil Brooks, 'The Judge and the Adversary System', *The Canadian Judiciary* 89 (A. Linden ed., 1976). For a very different approach, *see* David Barnhizer, 'The Virtue of Ordered Conflict: A Defense of the Adversary System', 79 *Neb. L. Rev.* 657 (2000).

win ... is often only incidentally, or coincidentally, if at all, a service to the public interest'.[21]

Nevertheless, it is highly likely that the adversary system will remain a staple feature of the legal process in the near to middle future. It is simply not possible to predict with any confidence that the adversary system will be abandoned or substantially moderated in the next few decades. While there have been numerous initiatives to mollify and accommodate the distorting impact of the adversarial process (e.g., increased arbitration, mandated mediation, intensive negotiation), they tend to react to and maintain the adversarial dynamic that is at the heart of the legal process. Consequently, any proposal to reformulate legal ethics must do so within the significant confines and milieu of the adversary system.

The upshot of this is that any effort to present ethical lawyers as anything other than adversaries, albeit in a more sophisticated and less bellicose style, is unrealistic and utopian. If it were possible to do away with the adversary system, then the present state of legal ethics and its transformation would be so much less daunting and so much more achievable. As things stand, therefore, a different approach to legal ethics must be capable of functioning within the general framework of the adversary system. The ethical lawyer must be able to be ethical in the existing legal process, dominated as it is by the adversary system, not in some idealized future. To pretend otherwise is to succumb to an unrealizable romanticism. The challenge for legal ethicists is a constrained one – to think about how lawyers can be adversarial and ethical at the same time.

While this all may seem to add up to a gloomy outlook for any initiative to develop a new theory and practice of legal ethics, there is no need for despondency. Contrary to accepted wisdom, nothing about the adversary system demands the extreme form of 'zealous advocacy' or 'hired gunmanship' that has become accepted and associated with it. It remains entirely possible for lawyers to be adversaries and still act ethically; the ethical adversary is not an oxymoron. While the adversary system places certain constraints on lawyers and asks them to play a strongly differentiated professional

[21] Marvin Frankel, 'The Search for Truth: An Umpireal View', 123 *U. Pa. La. Rev.* 1031, 1055 (1975).

role, there is still ample scope to move beyond the imagery and stylings of the hired gun. There is no moral compunction to represent clients in ways that require lawyers to lie and cheat or that condone underhanded and sharp practices. Indeed, there are strong ethical and professional reasons for not doing so. To be an adversary is not to abandon ethics, but to reframe them within a particular context of social engagement.

In a similar vein, it can be insisted that there is nothing about the adversary system that requires lawyers to put the interests of any particular client or their own representation of those interests above the public interest. Once it is conceded that the dilution of the public interest to the amoral or neutral serving of clients' interests, whether just or unjust in character and effect, is neither required nor desirable, it becomes possible to begin the task of placing legal ethics on a much more secure and ethically cogent basis. Committed to justice and the Rule of Law, legal professionals will be better positioned to provide a more telling riposte to Macaulay's jibe about 'whether it be right that a [lawyer] should, with a wig on his head, and a band round his neck, do for a guinea what, without these appendages, he would think it wicked and infamous to do for an empire'.[22] Unless today's lawyers have a more convincing answer to that striking interrogative, then legal ethicists, including me, will have failed in their responsibility to develop and defend a theory and practice of legal ethics worthy of the name.

CONCLUSION

It is my contention, therefore, that such a sustained riposte to the defenders of the traditional or standard conception is not only desirable, but also possible. Even within the adversarial and, at times, warlike context of contemporary lawyering, it is feasible to work out and justify a revised and revitalized version of what it means to be an ethical lawyer. Accordingly, rather than simply offer a spruced-up apology for the status quo and the conventional understandings of ethical professional conduct, I will demonstrate

[22] Thomas Babington Macaulay, *Critical and Historical Essays Contributed to the Edinburgh Review* 312 (1877).

that a new and imaginative model of the adversarial lawyer is realizable. Moreover, I will insist that such a professional image can explain the existence of a clear division between lawyers' personal and professional ethical roles as well as indicate the scope, the content and the details of such a professional role.

To do this, I will turn to an exploration of how the shift from treating lawyers as hired guns to envisaging them as warriors or military-like officers might pay handsome, if unexpected, ethical dividends. While the exploration of the ethics of warfare might seem like a strange and unpromising detour, I will show how a substantial appreciation of military ethics can contribute to a genuine bolstering of the appeal and force of legal ethics in an adversarial system. Indeed, the turn to military ethics is much more promising than other recent efforts to reinvigorate legal ethics.[23] Also, by going down this particular reconstructive road, there is a chance to vindicate fully Justice John Gibson's 1845 opinion that 'it is a popular, but gross mistake to suppose that a lawyer owes no fidelity to anyone except his client [who is] the keeper of his professional conscience.'[24] In contrast to the pinched and barren vision of Wendel and others, such a new departure might be exactly the fillip that is needed. Furthermore, so rejuvenated, ethical lawyers might be better able to fulfill their professional responsibilities as not merely operatives of the legal process, but as genuine participants in the administration of *justice*.

[23] In particular, it is much more preferable to the resort to economic analysis as a potential way to salvage the flagging efforts of traditional scholarship. *See* Randal Graham, *Legal Ethics* (2005) (presents legal ethics from an explicitly economic point of view). *See also* Richard W. Painter, 'Rules Lawyers Play By', 76 *N.Y.U. L. Rev.* 665 (2001) (uses economic theory to demonstrate general trends in professional responsibility rules); George M. Cohen, 'When Law and Economics Met Professional Responsibility', 67 *Fordham L. Rev.* 273 (1998) (treats professional responsibility as an effort to minimize agency costs); Larry E. Ribstein, Symposium, 'Ethical Rules, Agency Costs, and Law Firm Structure', 84 *Va. L. Rev.* 1707 (1998) (ethical rules as a way to reduce lawyer-client agency costs); Jonathan R. Macey & Geoffrey P. Miller, 'An Economic Analysis of Conflict of Interest Regulation', 82 *Iowa L. Rev.* 965 (1997) (modeling the attorney-client relationship as an agency contract).

[24] *Rush v. Cavenaugh*, 2 Pa. 187 (1845).

5

Taking War Ethically

The contemporary literature on military ethics has a long and rich pedigree. Anchored in the work of the ancient Greeks and Chinese, it was initiated in the Middle Ages and has come to maturity in contemporary treatises on modern warfare. Major contributions have been made by philosophers as distinct and distinguished as Sun Tzu, Saint Augustine, Saint Thomas Aquinas, Francisco de Victoria, Francisco Suarez, Hugo Grotius and Immanuel Kant. The common thread has been the effort to reflect on and formulate the legitimate principles for determining the *whys*, *whens* and *hows* of war: Why should war be begun? When should war be declared? How should war be waged and terminated? Not surprisingly, in answering these questions, the philosophical field of military ethics is suitably contested.[1] This means that, as with any project of ethical reflection, the 'just war' tradition should be thought of as constantly evolving and changing, not as forever fixed and definitive.

THE MILITARY TRADITION

Whatever the case in love, all is not fair in war. And it is most decidedly not the case that anything goes. Military ethics is not beholden to or exhausted by the permissive mandate to win at all costs. The professional soldier or warrior is very much part of 'a

[1] *See* Peter Temes, *The Just War* (2003); *Just War in Comparative Perspective* (Paul Robinson ed., 2003); Brian Orend, *The Morality of War* (2006).

world of permissions and prohibitions – a moral world'.[2] Even in the exacting conditions of warfare, military personnel are considered situated within a moral context that both empowers them and controls them: they are to act as professionals who place ethical honor above material, instrumental or territorial gain. Accordingly, as objectionable as war is, many military ethicists and commentators maintain that it can be waged in ways that can be evaluated as morally better or worse. Indeed, as in most realms of moral argument and action, the energizing imperative is that the more serious and extensive the effects of chosen actions, the more compelling the ethical justifications for them need to be. As Michael Walzer notes, 'for war is the hardest place: if comprehensive and consistent moral judgments are possible there, they are possible everywhere.'[3]

Within the ethics of warfare, this overriding moral worldview and aspiration influences and shapes both the ends and means of military action. In mapping this ethical terrain, important distinctions have been made between and within three distinct areas of study:

- the conditions and arguments that can justify recourse to war (*jus ad bellum*);
- the moral requirements for the fair prosecution of war (*jus in bello*); and
- the just terms under which war should be halted (*jus post bellum*).

Even though the literature is fraught with disagreement at all levels of analysis and prescription, a rich body of discursive resources has been constructed that can be called on and deployed by ethical protagonists to tackle problems and dilemmas in starting, waging and ending war. Although it does not provide definitive answers, this oeuvre does provide a general framework within which issues can be debated and aired. Indeed, for present purposes, it can be reported that, even if military ethics is ultimately found wanting, it offers much more than the present theory and practice of legal ethics does in addressing the ethical conundrums and conditions for engaging in legal or adversarial action.

[2] Michael Walzer, *Just and Unjust Wars: A Moral Argument with Historical Illustrations* 36 (3rd ed. 2000).

[3] *Id.* at xxv.

As can be expected of a mature and balanced ethical theory, military ethics adopts a positive as well as negative tone in its exhortations and demands.[4] The ethical soldier is produced by the injunctions of military ethics as much as held in check by them; ethical theory does not reduce ethical behavior to a list of prohibitions such that what is not forbidden is permissible. Indeed, it is important to understand that the 'expert' in war is not a 'lover of war'. The wise and responsible military leader or warrior is one who works hard to avoid war and its ensuing and inevitable degradations. However, if war is inevitable, she takes up hostilities not only with a genuine reluctance, but also with a deep commitment to acting honorably. Indeed, the problem of motivating ethical behavior among combat troops has a much better prospect of success if a 'personal identity based on the virtues of chivalry and martial honor' can be developed rather than requiring a rote observance of restrictive rules, principles and the like.[5] A worthy ethical theory is one that inspires as well as inhibits actions and motivations in the name of the 'good soldier'.

Accordingly, at their best, members of the military are thoroughly and inescapably ethical beings. Soldiers are not simply constrained by a set of moral precepts. To assume otherwise is to suggest that soldiers are all Hobbesian savages – 'solitary, poor, nasty, brutish, and short'[6] – unless kept under tight institutional and ethical rein. Instead, it is more persuasive to see soldiers and officers as ordinary people, more and less moral by disposition and acculturation, who inhabit a professional role constructed by a commitment to a set of affirmative values and positive expectations. It is not so much that military personnel divest themselves of any moral sensibility in the service of some larger social objective, but that they take on different, but related ethical personae in their professional pursuits than they adopt and realize in their personal lives. Again, as Walzer insists, 'some sense of military honor is still the creed of the professional soldier.'[7]

[4] *See* Michael Ignatieff, 'Ethics and the New War', 2 *Canadian Mil. J.* 5 (Winter 2001).

[5] Mark Osiel, *Obeying Orders: Atrocity, Military Discipline, and the Law of War* 23 (1999).

[6] Thomas Hobbes, *Leviathan* ch. 13, para. 9 (1651).

[7] Walzer, *supra* note 2 at 34.

A PROFESSIONAL PURSUIT

There are many parallels between military personnel and lawyers. The most important is the fact that they both consider themselves part of a profession. As such, they not only maintain a certain level of specialized education and collective identity, but they ostensibly undertake their roles and obligations in the name of a more honorable and public set of purposive goals: they consider themselves beholden and accountable to more than their own cumulative private benefit or personal advancement. At its most ideal, military personnel and lawyers both claim a vital public dimension to their professional actions; the demands of personal sacrifice and collective discipline are justified as being in the service of a compelling and broader social commitment.[8] For soldiers and warriors, this is especially significant when they are asked to wage war and/or engage in front-line action.

Moreover, as professionals, both military personnel and lawyers accept that their ethical role as professionals is differentiated in important ways from their personal morals. Both lawyers and soldiers are not only expected, but also occasionally obliged to do things that might not be considered ethical in a private capacity. Of course, soldiers are authorized to maintain a much larger gap between their professional and personal roles. While lawyers might be authorized to lie and cheat in some circumstances, soldiers might well be obligated to kill and injure others as part of their professional mission in warfare. Nevertheless, while each occupies a strongly differentiated professional role, it is not a fully or completely differentiated role.[9] In order to engage in such extreme acts,

[8] *See* Samuel P. Huntington, *The Soldier and the State* 7 (1957) ('the modern officer corps is a professional body and the modern military officer is a professional man'); Malham M. Wakin, 'Professional Integrity', in *The Leader's Imperative* 95 (J. Carl Ficarrotta ed., 2001). Of course, not all commentators accept this high moral tone. Some maintain that military ethics represents a self-serving rationalization for a culture of violence and blind obedience. *See, for example*, Martin L. Cook, *The Moral Warrior* (2004).

[9] *See* Anthony E. Hartle, *Moral Issues in Military Decision Making* 7–9, 29–30 and 162–72 (2nd ed. 2004). As Hartle notes, 'the fundamental values that generate moral rules requiring general members of society to act one way in normal day-to-day life might call for lawyers to act quite differently in their professional role. Understanding that the profession of arms has a similar role-differentiated character can help clarify the moral nature of the professional military ethic.' *Id.* at 7.

members of the military are expected to conform to an ethical code of professional conduct. Being involved in war, even if highly and generally justified, does not give the military free rein to do what they want, to whom they want and when they want.

In sustaining any analogy between the institutional settings and ethical demands on lawyers and military personnel, it is important to be mindful of the differences in context as well as the similarities. Insofar as there is a strong ethical component to military service, it is important to distinguish the different responsibilities and roles accorded to different levels of military personnel. The first thing to note is that there is no useful or workable comparison between all lawyers and all military personnel. There are important distinctions to be made between officers and rank-and-file soldiers as regards their ethical obligations. Whereas soldiers are under strong legal, institutional and organizational pressure to follow the order of their superiors, senior officers have much greater leeway and responsibility to give orders to soldiers under their command that meet the ethical and legal guidelines that govern the exercise of military power.[10] Consequently, it is senior military officers who bear the most resemblance to lawyers in terms of their informing institutional context, individual decision making and structural dynamics.

Moreover, in order to appreciate the ethical and lawyer-equivalent role of such military personnel, it will also be necessary to pay close attention to the crucial dynamics and terms of the relationship between those senior commanders (e.g., chiefs of staff and regional commanders) and their civilian supervisors (e.g., secretary/minister of defense and secretary/minister of the army). This is the relational fulcrum of military ethics in a similar way that the lawyer-client relationship is in the realm of legal ethics. Like lawyers, commanding officers are beholden to the directions of civilian authorities; they are understood not to have the freedom to ignore or fail to follow the lawful requests of political superiors. While high-ranking military officers can and should represent the perspective of the military and advise the government about preferable courses of action, they

[10] This, of course, is not an absolute imperative. While the defense of 'superior orders' to otherwise criminal acts is extensive, it does have limits. For discussion of this regarding lawyers, *see infra* pp. 106–108.

are ultimately obliged to do the final bidding of the government as the elected representatives of the public.[11]

While there is a notional distinction between ends (civilian) and means (military), it is for civilian superiors to determine where that line should be drawn and, therefore, the jurisdictional independence of military officers. This civilian-military relationship is considered an important part of the governmental compact in a constitutional democracy. Political legitimacy is secured and promoted by the military arm of government being accountable to the elected representatives of the people. It can be appreciated, therefore, that there is a sufficient equivalence between the basic institutional and professional context of lawyers and military officers to make a viable and instructive analogy between them in terms of their ethical role and responsibilities.

There is potentially much to be learned about lawyers' professional responsibilities by examining the discourse and resources of military ethics. In particular, the military and legal professions share the similar challenge of determining whether their members have a duty to act exclusively in line with the interests and directions of their superiors, be it clients or officials: May or should lawyers and military commanders possess and exercise a certain professional ethical autonomy that might put them in conflict with those who have putative authority over them? This dilemma cuts to the heart of the professional compact in both law and military service. While there might not be an exact fit between legal and military ethics, there is a sufficient analogy to warrant a fruitful look at one in light of the other.

MERCENARIES AND LAWYERS

While not all lawyers are the same in terms of their professional role, institutional allegiance and ethical self-awareness, neither are soldiers. An important distinction has to be made between those

[11] *See* Samuel Huntington, *The Soldier and the State: The Theory and Politics of Civil-Military Relations* (1957). *See also* Carl Ceulemans & Guy van Damme, 'The Soldier and the State: An Analysis of Samuel Huntington's View on Military Obedience Toward Political Authority', 10 *Prof. Ethics* 7 (2002); George R. Lucas Jr., 'Advice and Dissent: "The Uniform Perspective"' 8 *J. Mil. Ethics* 141 (2009). For a strong challenge to traditional definitions, *see* Tony Lynch & A. J. Walsh, 'The Good Mercenary'? 8 *J. Pol. Phil.* 133 (2000).

soldiers who are members of a state's armed forces and those who are not – mercenaries. Whether a soldier is one or the other has significant implications for her legal, professional and moral standing and regulation. While the line is far from easy to draw in any definitive or fixed way, it is possible to make some important generalizations that shape and color the ethical and professional landscape. A mercenary is one kind of soldier, but not all soldiers are mercenaries.

A mercenary is considered a professional combatant who is hired to complete a certain job rather than be enlisted as a member of a state's armed forces. Although there will be many reasons for taking on such a role, a primary motivation will be private financial gain; a sense of adventure or derring-do might be another. In recent decades, the use of private military corporations (PMCs) to provide a variety of services traditionally done by the armed forces has grown enormously and transformed the role and importance of mercenaries.[12] These mercenaries are to be contrasted with the so-called honorable soldier who is treated as being committed to some goal that is not exclusively or primarily materialistic. Honorable soldiers are knowledgeable about war in both its operational and reflective dimensions, they respect the value of human life, and they are self-conscious about their moral responsibilities as soldiers.[13] While both these characterizations are very stylistic and polarized, they do capture some valuable and revealing differences between mercenaries and military personnel.

The very term 'mercenary' in modern parlance signifies something morally dubious and ignoble; there is nothing honorable

[12] The literature on mercenaries is vast. *See, for example*, Anthony Mockler, *The Mercenaries* (1969); W. Burchett & D. Roebuck, *The Whores of War* (1977); Janice E. Thomson, *Mercenaries, Pirates, and Sovereigns* (1994); David Shearer, *Private Armies and Military Intervention* (1998); Sarah Percy, *Mercenaries* (2007). On PMCs, *see* Shearer, *supra*; *Private Military and Security Companies* (Andrew Alexandra, Deane-Peter Baker & Marina Caparini eds., 2008).

[13] Joseph Runzo, 'Benevolence, Honourable Soldiers and Private Military Companies: Reformulating Just War Theory', in *Private Military and Security Companies: Ethics, Policies and Civil Military Relations*, 56 at 66 (Andrew Alexandra, Deane-Peter Baker & Marina Caparini, eds., 2008). *See also* Protocol Additional to the Geneva Conventions of 12 August 1949, and relating to the Protection of Victims of International Armed Conflicts (Protocol 1), art. 47, 8 June 1977, 1125 U.N.T.S. 3 [hereinafter Geneva Protocol].

or admirable about it. For instance, in the sixteenth-century *The Prince*, even Machiavelli rails against mercenaries, whom he considers 'useless and dangerous ... for they are disunited, ambitious, without discipline, unfaithful; bold among friends, among enemies cowardly; no fear of God, no faith with men'.[14] Little seems to have changed. Contemporary academic and popular opinion tends to unite in emphasizing the moral and institutional shortcomings of mercenaries, especially in the deceptively legitimate form of PMCs – they have different interests and priorities than the state; they are not directly responsible to military commanders and can be difficult to monitor; and they are more tempted to 'cut corners'.[15] However, they remain an increasingly used resource and familiar feature on the landscape of modern warfare. A particular appeal of PMCs is the fact that, under many Western constitutional schemes in regard to the waging of war, the executive branch of governments can circumvent some institutional control by legislatures and gain direct control over the placing and monitoring of such outsourcing arrangements. Such an end-run arrangement does little to instill any greater confidence in the roles and responsibilities of mercenaries or PMCs.

As criticized as it is, the role of mercenaries bears a considerable and unsettling resemblance to the general orientation of private lawyers; what is exceptional and marginal in military matters appears to be almost the rule in legal circles. While government lawyers and in-house counsel tend to be in different organizational situations, most private lawyers have a relationship with their clients that is very similar to that of mercenaries, not soldiers. The imagery of the hired gun is, of course, evocative of such a characterization. Lawyers do the bidding of their clients in exchange for payment, with no real questions asked. If clients can no longer

[14] Niccolò Machiavelli, *The Prince* 48 (Harvey C. Mansfield trans., 2nd ed. 1998) (1532).

[15] *See, for example*, Peter Warren Singer, *Corporate Warriors* (2003). However, the literature is not uniformly condemnatory. Some contend that there is much hypocrisy in this debate. The line between mercenaries and members of the armed forces in terms of motivation and performance is much blurrier than admitted. The term 'mercenary' is not necessarily morally indefensible, even if many of its operatives are. *See, for example*, Lynch & Walsh, *supra* note 11.

pay, then lawyers are generally entitled to withdraw their services and seek new clients.[16] Like mercenaries, lawyers have no necessary commitment to the cause of their clients or its moral valence. Indeed, as long as the clients' cause is not obviously unlawful, the lawyer is encouraged not to take a moral stand on that cause.

In a telling justificatory move within the traditional or standard conception, lawyers can even take moral pride in their studied indifference to the client's cause.[17] While lawyers can claim to be operating under the guidance of a higher cause (i.e., the Rule of Law), this turns out to be a rather shallow and circular explanation – the claim that lawyers actually adopt and conform to the role of amoral technician or hired gun is itself highly contentious. Moreover, this defense of legal ethics draws on a very thin and contested rendition of the Rule of Law.[18] For many, a commitment to the Rule of Law cannot be divorced from a reliance on some protection for certain basic human values and freedoms. By depicting the Rule of Law as being only about procedural justice and not substantive justice, lawyers compound the very problem that legal ethics is supposed to resolve – it casts ethical behavior as little more than conformity to law without any real attention paid to the worthiness of any particular laws or process. This is tantamount to contending that lawyers can act ethically in even the most heinous or abominable legal system, like Nazi Germany or Apartheid South Africa, by simply following the extant rules of law.

In adopting a professional stance of amoral loyalty to clients and their causes, the analogy with mercenaries seems much too close for comfort. By being more like mercenaries than military personnel, lawyers run the considerable risk of being condemned rather than celebrated for their moral detachment and ethical indifference. However, the upshot is even more depressing from the point of view

[16] *See Model Rules of Prof'l Conduct* R. 1.16(b) (2002); *CBA Code of Prof'l Conduct* ch. XII (2009); *SRA Code of Conduct* 2011 ch. 1 (2013).

[17] *See supra* Chapter 4. It is worth noting that, while doctors adopt a similar ethic of indifference to their patients' moral worth or causes of ill health, they are engaged in delivering a set of services whose overall goal (i.e., healing people) is more self-evidently worthy of ethical approval and support. *See, for example*, Hippocratic Oath; World Medical Association, Declaration of Geneva.

[18] *See generally* A. Hutchinson and P. Monahan, *The Rule of Law: Ideal or Ideology?* (1987).

of the ethical standing of the legal profession. As a result of sustained criticism of the role and use of mercenaries in warfare, there is now a large amount of commentary and regulation that places significant moral constraints on the actions of mercenaries; they no longer work entirely outside the reach of ethical surveillance and discipline. There are organizations and codes of conduct devoted to regulating and policing the activities of mercenaries and PMCs; the challenge is found in implementing and enforcing such regulations. Moreover, these moral constraints are far from minimal and go beyond the similar moral constraints that the law and professional bodies place on lawyers. For example, even PMCs are said to have a moral duty to third parties to avoid collateral damage and to respect the interests of third parties. Ironically, therefore, mercenaries operate in a more regulated ethical environment than lawyers do: the good mercenary is almost less the oxymoron than the good lawyer.

BEYOND THE HIRED GUN

It does not follow from the abandonment of the imagery and rhetoric of the hired gun or its mercenary equivalent that any assertive or aggressive depiction of lawyers is beyond the pale. As with so much else, it is more a matter of degree and emphasis. It is the force of my argument that it is possible to modulate and adjust the prevailing imagery so that it respects the adversarial context of litigation and, at the same time, introduces an honorable and substantively just dimension to the practice of litigation. This can be done by shifting the imagery and rhetoric from the hired gun to the warrior. As I will elaborate, this involves a less mercenary and more noble vision of combat. Because conflict is and will continue to be at the heart of litigation, any viable reform of legal ethics must recognize and incorporate that feature into its enabling and informing premises. Consequently, acting ethically as a litigation lawyer is less about not 'fighting' and more about fighting fairly.

This elusive and nontraditional alternative to the traditional persona of the hired gun can be most expressively captured by the notion and practice of being a 'warrior'. This imagery stands in sharp contrast to the hired gun. While the hired gun is all business and function, warriors are as much concerned with honor and moral worth in how they go about their tasks as anything else. They recognize and defend the idea that the ambition is not simply to win, but to fight fair and to take defeat, if it happens, as a necessary cost of being honorable. They eschew the understanding that their role is simply a means to an end. Instead, they portray themselves as part of a vocation and a profession. Because warriors need to hold onto their basic humanity and professional self-respect in battle conditions, their code 'is a kind of moral and psychological armor that protects the warrior from becoming a monster in his or her own eyes'.[19] Whereas the hired gun affects a studied indifference (or worse) to the moral niceties and subtleties of fighting for no cause greater than their employers' or clients' interests, the warrior is committed to a greater good than mere victory or material reward. Warriors inhabit their own strict and demanding moral universe; the hired gun does not.

Some will be tempted to dismiss this kind of distinction between hired guns and warriors as lacking any real import or depth; each is a fighter and any efforts to present them as something more are only so much window dressing. This criticism is often tied to a larger rejection of fighting and military *spirit de corps* as definitively masculine and as escalating to an almost *machismo* degree.[20] However, while this offers an important caution, it does not work to undermine entirely the warrior image as a defensible character of ethical combat. As a matter of substance, the warrior notion actually factors in a variety of considerations that are fundamental to the care-based, feminist conception of legal theory.[21] It is less that

[19] Shannon French, *The Code of the Warrior* 10 (2003). *See also* David Barnhizer, 'The Virtue of Ordered Conflict: A Defense of the Adversary System', 79 *Neb. L. Rev.* 657 (2000).

[20] *See* Michael Grossberg, 'Institutionalizing Masculinity: The Law as a Masculine Profession', in *Meanings for Manhood* 133, 134 (Mark C. Carnes & Clyde Griffen eds., 1990) ('masculinity was so fundamental to the profession's consciousness that for most of the century it acted as an unarticulated first principle').

[21] *See* Carol Gilligan, *In a Different Voice* (1982); Carrie Menkel-Meadow, 'Portia in a Different Voice: Speculations on a Woman's Lawyering Process', 1 *Berkeley Women's L.J.* 39 (1985); Erica Rackley, 'From Arachne to Charlotte: An Imaginative Revisiting of Gilligan's in a Different Voice', 13 *Wm. & Mary J. Women & L.* 751 (2007).

combat occurs and more that it must be a last resort. However, once combat ensues, the warrior will remain committed to fighting fairly and with due care for the other party to the dispute; there is no fighting for fighting's sake. Moreover, there is a relatively rich tradition of female warriors in both history and literature – Athena, Boudicca, Jeanne d'Arc, the *Aeneid*'s Camilla, Maeve of Connaught and even Xena, Nikita and Buffy of TV fame. Each of these characters offers a discernible and significant ethically infused complexity in contrast to the amoral and one-dimensional world of the hired gun.

Accordingly, the idea of the warrior, whatever its perceived or real failings in practice, makes it a viable and alternative model for lawyers in search of a more ethical role model. It suggests that professional esteem is about more than winning cases and causes. Instead, it recommends an attitude and approach that is ethical in scope and substance; it takes very seriously the quality of fairness and honor. Warriors strive to be dignified in all they do and to work for a greater good than temporary success; they are in the game of glory, albeit more humbly pursued. As Dr. Johnson put it, honor is all about 'nobility of soul, magnanimity, and a scorn of meanness'.[22] Although this imagery can be overplayed and used as a cover for decidedly unheroic behavior, the warrior mentality does recommend a certain respect for oneself and others; it resonates with the professional codes of lawyers' duties to act with courage, integrity, good faith, justice and dignity.[23] Their moral universe does not begin and end with the leaders' or their own interests; warriors are open and responsive to a broader set of social and ethical concerns.

SOME CAVEATS

As with any exercise in analogical analysis, the strength of the intellectual device to be used is found as much in its limits as in its central insight. It is vitally important, therefore, to emphasize not only military ethics' illuminating strength and suggestive possibilities, but also its explanatory boundaries and distortive effects when applied to legal ethics. Accordingly, I should add a few important

[22] Samuel Johnson, *A Dictionary of the English Language* (1755).

[23] *See Model Rules of Prof'l Conduct* pmbl. (2002); *CBA Code of Prof'l Conduct* pmbl., ch. 1 (2009); *SRA Code of Conduct* 2011 Principles (2013).

caveats about any attempt to analogize military ethics and legal ethics. While I maintain that there are sufficient similarities between the ethical challenges of law and military practice to warrant serious comparison and cross-fertilization, I am not suggesting that the legal and military terrains are exactly the same or that their ethical dimensions and dilemmas are the same. Important differences must be identified and noted if this comparative enterprise is to be helpful and productive. However, there is more that is similar than different in their comparison.

Perhaps most importantly, the main challenge to a persuasive and productive comparison between military ethics and legal ethics is that the stakes in military engagements and in legal conflicts are very different; they are much higher in war than in litigation. At its most blunt and direct, soldiers risk their lives and take the lives of others; lawyers do not. Because of this, it is contended that the ethical pressures and moral constraints on soldiers are justified in being much stronger and more demanding than on lawyers. Whereas lawyers are involved in serious and important work, litigation has less deleterious social impact and human consequences than war and, therefore, the role of lawyers needs less justification. In short, the public interest demands that soldiers must be kept on a much tighter ethical leash than lawyers because the damage that lawyers wreak is much less grave and disturbing. It is because the stakes for individuals and society are higher on the battlefield that the ethics of war are and should, according to critics, be more demanding than legal ethics.

Nevertheless, although there is some force and logic to this criticism, it is not at all as telling or as damning as many might at first think. One response is a practical one. Sometimes, particularly in the criminal setting, the stakes are as equally high as in the military context in that they do include the possibilities of life and death. In such circumstances, there are already significant constraints and responsibilities on prosecutors (as opposed to criminal defense lawyers) in the name of the public interest and in consequence of the fact that serious matters of personal liberty are in play. Also, the stakes are extremely high in much family litigation where the quality and fate of children's lives, for example, might be on the line: the likely costs of excessive zeal or unethical behavior by lawyers on behalf of their clients in such instances are especially damaging for the families involved and for society at large. So, while the stakes in litigation might not be quite as high as in war, they are far from trifling or less deserving of professional discipline. Moreover, the importance of law to the public and society generally suggests that it is important that, insofar as lawyers play a vital role in lawmaking and social regulation through litigation, lawyers are obliged to act in accordance with the demands of the public interest.

Another response is more principled. Although there are genuine dissimilarities between the activities of lawyers in litigation and soldiers in war, they both rely on an analytical structure that draws on the justificatory tools of 'professional role' and 'the public interest'. This might well lead to differences in emphasis and nuance around the application of these tools, but it does not lead to any decisive split in the ethical road to be traveled. Both legal ethics and military ethics work much the same analytical street. They each give extensive powers to lawyers and soldiers to do harm that would otherwise be condemned as unethical and unacceptable if it were done outside their professional role and not in the public interest. In this way, the justificatory structures are sufficiently similar in ambition, even if they are not identical in application. Consequently, this means that, while there is ample reason to compare the two, the effort to apply military ethics to lawyers' work must be done with a sensitive appreciation of the differences between the professional undertakings of military personnel and lawyers.

Accordingly, lawyers are not soldiers, but they are professionals who work under comparable conditions and who can benefit from similar analytical frameworks of ethical justification and professional sanction. In the same way that military warriors should care about the human toll that they exact, so should lawyers care about the social and human consequences of litigation. The paramount need to act honorably can guide both lawyers and soldiers in fulfilling their public responsibilities. Of course, not all wars or military engagements are the same; there are many different kinds of war and warfare. Conventional wars between states are not the same as state efforts to combat guerilla warfare or terrorists attacks. Nevertheless, with suitable allowance for context, military ethics (and, by extension, legal ethics) can adapt itself. Neither military ethics nor legal ethics comprises a one-size-fits-all regimen. Instead, they both offer broad frameworks that can accommodate and handle different settings and demands. If they were not so equipped, they would not comprise much of a serious or sustainable ethical resource for any professional enterprise.

It might also be added that a battlefield, unlike a court, is a place where individuals not only put their lives at risk, but also are asked to exhibit genuine bravery and selfless devotion to the cause of a just war. This is obviously not true of lawyers; their participation involves less valiant behavior and personal sacrifice.[24] Nevertheless, while lawyers are not at physical risk, some are willing to put their professional and personal reputations on the line to advance a particular case or cause. This sense of laudable, if not heroic commitment by some lawyers should not be discounted or underestimated entirely. In short, lawyers and soldiers are both sometimes asked to make sacrifices for others: that one is of a higher order than the other is not definitive in assessing its comparative weight or worth.

Finally, in recommending the suggestive potential of military ethics for fructifying the professional practice of legal ethics, I am not making any claims at all about the actual performance of military ethics in real-world situations: many critical rejoinders make the point that the precepts of military ethics are more honored in their breach than in their observance.[25] Indeed, the just war tradition might well operate as much as an ideology as anything else; soldiers might be only too willing to believe that all chosen ends are just or that the ends justify the means. Indeed, sadly, it may well be that unjust wars and unjust ways of waging them are the practical norm. Some critics go so far as to contend that just war rhetoric actually breeds violence: appeals to justice and morality galvanize soldiers to carry out actions that they might not and should not otherwise do.[26]

However, whether the gap between the theory and practice of military ethics is large or small, it makes no difference to the

[24] Alec Walen, 'Criticizing the Obligatory Acts of Lawyers: A Response to Markovits's Legal Ethics from the Lawyer's Point of View', 16 *Yale J.L. & Human.* 1 (2004).

[25] *See, for example, The Leader's Imperative supra* note 8; Cook, *supra* note 8; Andrew Fiala, *The Just War Myth* (2008).

[26] Laurie Calhoun, 'The Meta-ethical Paradox of Just War Theory', 4 *Ethical Theory and Moral Practice* 41 (2001).

legitimacy of my appeal to the philosophical discourse of military ethics as a helpmate for legal ethics. That said, early reflections suggest that there is much to be gained from a more comprehensive effort to explore legal ethics through the lens of the 'ethics of warfare'. By doing so, it might become possible to transform and improve the theory and practice of legal ethics. Of course, as with any interdisciplinary analysis of this kind, caution will need to be exercised in ensuring that the different as well as similar aspects of law-fare and warfare are thoroughly canvassed. Moreover, any analysis will need to be sensitive to the (dis)connection between stated professional ethics and actual professional practice in both military and legal contexts.

Nevertheless, it is worth emphasizing that any scheme of professional ethics is ultimately only as good as its acceptance and adoption by its practitioners. Practice might not make perfect, but it will oblige lawyers to put their professional money where their ethical mouth is. Like with soldiers, it is more persuasive to see lawyers as ordinary people, more and less moral by disposition and acculturation, who inhabit a professional role constructed by a commitment to a set of affirmative values and positive expectations. Again, like soldiers, it is not so much that lawyers should divest themselves of any personal moral sensibility in the service of some larger social objective. Instead, lawyers must be prepared to take on different, but related ethical personae in their professional pursuits than they adopt and realize in their personal lives. At its best, one will reinforce and complement the other as part of a larger ethical whole.

CONCLUSION

With those caveats in mind, I maintain that it is useful and credible to rejig professional legal ethics to be more in line with military ethics. Of course, the analysis that follows is offered by way of suggestion and experimentation. Nevertheless, notwithstanding that, I do insist that the ethics of warfare has much to recommend it in developing and detailing an ethical posture that is, at a minimum, a vast improvement on the present state of theory and practice in legal ethics and professional responsibility. Resort to military ethics can set in motion a reflective process that will add an aspirational as well as hands-on element to the study of legal ethics and professional responsibility. Military ethics has much to teach lawyers who seek a more compelling and justified account of what makes lawyers more ethical and deserving of the large powers that they are granted and exercise in the name of the greater public interest. The good soldier and the good lawyer are united in their dedication to leading a fulfilling and honorable life in service of the public interest.

6

In the Name of Just Ends

In understanding and evaluating what people do, it is important to appreciate the larger context and circumstances in which they act. What will be appropriate in one situation may not be acceptable in another. Although there might well be some ways of acting that are treated as immoral in all circumstances (e.g., torture?), few take the view that certain actions are irredeemably and always unethical outside the context in which they are taken. For instance, while telling lies may be generally frowned upon as an approved course of moral conduct, it may be deemed permissible and even encouraged in certain extreme situations where the consequences of not telling lies are particularly draconian (e.g., life and death). In more strictly philosophical terms, this references the contested relation between means and ends: In what circumstances do certain ends justify the use of certain means that might otherwise be thought unethical? This conundrum is at the heart of any ethical debate. Not surprisingly, it has particular salience for the application of military ethics in the area of legal ethics and professional responsibility.

GOING TO WAR

Not all wars are created equal. The Just War tradition is built on the bedrock stance that there is and must be a distinction between just and unjust wars. However, as with all ethical traditions, there is a continuing and heated debate within the 'just war' community about the precise conditions that must be satisfied to justify recourse to war if an ethical imprimatur is to be given to its prosecution and continuance.[1] Nevertheless, although there is controversy about their precise meaning and scope, the basic criteria seem to be generally agreed upon. There are five conditions and each must be satisfied for a war to be considered just:

(1) **A Just Cause** – The evaluation about whether there is a just cause is to be made at the time war is started and with an understanding of the parties' reasonable expectations. The range of acceptable reasons has narrowed in recent decades to include only grave and aggressive threats to large groups or populations; this may or may not include the violation of basic human rights. Intervention is usually restricted to the protection of innocent lives. Also, there are difficult questions to be asked about whether an anticipatory defense or preemptive strike is ever warranted.

(2) **Rightful Intentions** – To be justified, a war must be fought with honorable and candid motives, not ulterior or hidden ones. War cannot be waged simply to recapture things taken or punish people who have done wrong. The stated 'just cause' must be the sole or overriding justification, not a pretext for belligerent action.

(3) **Proportionality** – There must exist a balance between the good to be achieved by war and the inevitable harm to be done by its waging. This assessment must encompass all parties and territory, enemy and ally alike, to the conflict. Only if the benefits/good seem reasonably proportional to the costs/evil on an all-in basis may the war be begun and continued.[2]

(4) **Last Resort** – Hostilities are not to be commenced until and unless all else fails. War may only be waged, therefore, if all

[1] Brian Orend, *Just War Theory*, *Stanford Encyclopedia of Philosophy* (Edward N. Zalta ed., rev. ed. 2005), available at http://plato.stanford.edu/entries/war/. There is also much debate about what counts as 'war' for these purposes. *See* Steven Lee, *Ethics and War* 6–9 (2012); *Moral Constraints on War* (Bruno Coppieters & Nick Fotion eds., 2002); *Just War in Comparative Perspective* (Paul Robinson ed., 2003); *The Price of Peace* (Charles Reed & David Ryall eds., 2007). I will not deal with this here, but reserve discussion of this matter to the legal ethics context. *See infra* pp. 83–86.

[2] *See* Thomas Hurka, 'Proportionality in the Morality of War', 33 *Phil. & Pub. Aff.* 34, 38 (2005).

peaceful and reasonable alternatives for resolving the conflict have been tried and exhausted. In particular, this demands extensive recourse to diplomatic negotiation conducted in good faith and with practical intent.

(5) **Reasonable chance of success** – Because of the inevitable havoc and irreparable harm caused by going to war, hostilities can only be commenced if there exists some reasonable prospect that victory is possible. There is no mandate to wage war in a futile cause or where disproportionate measures are required to achieve success.

These interrelated requirements for the waging of a just war are based on the rebuttable presumption that war is to be avoided at almost all costs. While there are just and unjust wars, there are no truly welcome wars. Of course, because just war is essentially framed as a measured response to unjust aggression, it will rarely be the case that war can be just for both sides.[3] Nevertheless, there will be occasions on which each side to the conflict will claim that justice is on their side. Moreover, in such high-stakes affairs, there is unlikely to be any agreement on what is to count as 'just' in any definitive or final way. This applies equally to the theoretical community that has hemmed and hawed over what the precise demands of justice might be in particular circumstances and specific settings. This challenge is especially severe when nations and cultures clash.

Accordingly, just war theory does not provide any formulaic method for determining the justness of any particular proclamation of war. Instead, it provides a facilitative framework and set of discursive resources within and through which to address and argue about justness. As such, it offers itself as a suggestive example for legal ethics, especially its struggle to talk about and delineate what lawyers should and should not do in negotiating the puzzles and dilemmas that confront them in their daily professional activities. Indeed, with some obvious adjustments and reorientation, the ethics of warfare can help to plug the gaps left by traditional

[3] *See* Peter Lee, *Ethics and War: An Introduction* 77 (2012); Inis L. Claude, 'Just War: Doctrine and Institutions', 95 *Pol. Sci. Q.* 83, 87 (1980). History tells us that the victor has an uncanny capacity to proclaim *ex post facto* that victory has favored its cause.

theorizing about legal ethics and professional responsibility. Rather than remain aloof or indifferent to the ends and motivations of the clients they take and the causes they defend, lawyers must be prepared to take some, if constrained, ethical stance on such matters. This is particularly pressing and evident in the case of 'client selection', 'competence' and 'the decision to litigate'.

THE COMPANY WE KEEP

It is surely the case that there is no more important decision that affects lawyers' ethical commitments and behavior than the identity and causes of the clients that they take on. Once the lawyer-client relationship is established, much of the ethical die is cast. Lawyers are obliged to place their clients' interests ahead of others: 'as a professional person, one has a special care for the interests of those accepted as clients, just as his friends, his family, and he himself have a very general claim to his special concern.'[4] There is room for discussion about the extent and details of that primary commitment,[5] but its pivotal role is indisputable. Also, all clients are entitled to the same level of competence and commitment from their lawyers. Taking on clients and representing them in an incompetent or half-hearted way is a travesty of any kind of ethical or professional expectation.

As things stand, most jurisdictions in the common law world allow lawyers to choose to represent whichever clients they wish. While there is a general professional understanding that lawyers should not refuse clients lightly, there is neither a moral obligation to take on particular clients or causes nor a moral prohibition from taking on particular clients or causes (as long as the lawyer is competent to do so). Accordingly, although lawyers are granted special privileges and powers by virtue of their professional standing as lawyers, they retain considerable autonomy in how they use those privileges and powers: the importance of the public's need for legal

[4] Charles Fried, 'The Lawyer as Friend: The Moral Foundations of the Lawyer-Client Relation', 85 *Yale L.J.* 1060, 1067 (1976). *See Model Rules of Prof'l Conduct* R 1.3 cmt. para. 1 (2002); *CBA Code of Prof'l Conduct* ch. II (Can. 2009); *SRA Code of Conduct* 2011 Principles, ch. 1 (2013).

[5] *See infra* Chapter 7.

services does not entirely submerge lawyers' own sense of choice over who they work for and how they work for them. Although there is much rhetoric to the contrary, therefore, the traditional practice on client selection is that lawyers neither are under any obligation to take unpopular cases nor are they ethically compromised by the moral (un)worthiness of their clients' causes; the sins of clients are not to be visited upon their lawyers.[6] In the tradition account of lawyering, the need to provide counsel for everyone is understood to be a collective responsibility of the profession, not an individual mandate for each lawyer.

Of course, an application of military ethics recommends a very different approach. With its emphasis on 'just cause' and 'rightful intentions', there would exist a significantly greater requirement for lawyers to be much more concerned with the substantive justice of their clients' causes than presently exists or is expected. Client selection becomes a direct ethical undertaking and might, in some circumstances, not only permit lawyers to reject certain potential clients, but also demand that they do so. Such an approach takes seriously lawyers' general ethical injunction to act with 'integrity' and 'honour'.[7] Rather than affect a studied moral indifference, it suggests that lawyers make a moral assessment of their clients' plans and intentions. In this way, there should be certain compatibility between the goals of the client and the ethical orientation of the lawyer. Accordingly, while it is important that clients have a legal basis for action,[8] this is only a necessary, but not a sufficient condition for lawyers' involvement in their cases.

[6] *See, for example*, *Model Rules of Prof'l Conduct* R. 1.2 (b) ('A lawyer's representation of a client ... does not constitute an endorsement of the client's political, economic, social or moral views or activities'). Exception to this is the cab-rank rule of English barristers that requires them to take all clients. However, they still can refuse clients on the basis of professional competence and the client's impecuniosity. *See Code of Conduct of Bar of England and Wales* pt. VI, paras. 601–4.

[7] *See, for example*, *Model Rules of Prof'l Conduct* pmbl. (2002); *CBA Code of Prof'l Conduct* pmbl., ch. 1 (2009); *SRA Code of Conduct* 2001 Principles (2013).

[8] This legal standard for bringing non-frivolous actions has been difficult to define with any precision and even more difficult to police with any consistency. *See supra* Chapter 3.

An important corollary of this 'just cause' approach would be to encourage lawyers to talk to prospective clients and develop an ethical standard against which to evaluate whether the objective of the case or cause is worthy and whether the means that might be required will be allowed to be used. Moreover, this would imply that lawyers should treat their potential clients as moral persons capable of engaging in debate and changing. It is unrealistic to imagine or expect that every lawyer will, like Socrates, be guided only by the need to do right rather than wrong. Most lawyers are not unreasonably concerned about their jobs, paying their mortgages and providing for their children. Also, it is impractical to believe that lawyers and clients will have to share a whole ethical outlook on life to be able to establish a workable and moral professional relationship. It might be that lawyers will need to make an important distinction between their 'values' and their 'convictions'. For example, while lawyers might refuse to represent people associated with a particular side in the abortion struggle, they might not have any difficulty in representing such persons in unrelated property transactions.

As things presently stand, it is revealing to note that one of the only areas of legal practice in which there is genuine discussion about 'just causes' is clinical or poverty lawyering where remuneration is not generally tied to the success of the litigation or legal work. The basic tension is between those who contend that poverty law clinics, as they are often funded publicly, should take on all cases and those who argue that it is entirely acceptable that such clinics should be able to choose sides and only take on clients on one side.[9] For example, a clinic may decide to counsel and represent only victims, not perpetrators, of domestic abuse or tenants in disputes with their landlords. Mindful that many private lawyers often take a de facto position on the union or management side in labor relations and for plaintiffs or defendants in tort actions, publicly funded lawyers might surely be accorded the same leeway, especially when their reasons are principled and often benefit those who would otherwise go unrepresented.

[9] *See* Jennie Abell, 'Women, Violence, and the Criminal Law: "It's the Fundamentals of Being a Lawyer that Are at Stake Here"', 17 *Queen's L.J.* 147 (1992); Mary Jane Mossman, 'Gender Equality, Family Law, and Access to Justice', 8 *Int'l J.L. & Fam.* 357 (1994).

An interesting adoption of a broader 'just cause' stance is taken by Duncan Kennedy. He insists that the right not to take clients has a much wider moral ambit than simply refusing to represent people or organizations that lawyers think have evil intentions or whose activities are generally reviled. He maintains that lawyers should take full responsibility for the clients that they take and the causes they advance: it is ethically wrong to argue a case or a cause that will do more harm than good if lawyers think that their clients should not be in court in the first place or that clients should lose. In particular, lawyers should not represent clients who are using technical defenses to avoid justified liability or who are enforcing their valid legal rights in a bad cause. For Kennedy, 'you are tarred with bad actions of clients that you facilitate in your work as a lawyer.'[10] Working against/for unionization if a lawyer is pro/antiunion, or advising for the postponement/implementation of environmental controls if a lawyer is pro/anti-environmental rights is something that lawyers should not do. And they should not do it as a matter of professional ethical responsibility. This does not mean that lawyers should choose to represent only those clients whom they or anyone else would approve. It simply means that lawyers should represent only those clients or causes they are prepared to defend as being more, rather than less, beneficial for society.

The most obvious charges against such a substantive position are that lawyers will become the ethical gatekeepers of the legal process and that some persons will go without legal representation. As regards the first charge, while lawyers would seem ill suited to such a role, it would seem that this control function is already largely the case. Lawyers' choices about the clients and causes to be served are already dictated and driven by their own interests, especially economic and subject-specific ones. Although the ethical considerations in play are more indirect and veiled, they do significantly impact the allocation and availability of legal services. At least, a 'just cause' would bring these ethical considerations out of the institutional shadows and make them more amenable to enlightened analysis and discussion.

[10] Duncan Kennedy, 'The Responsibility of Lawyers for the Justice of Their Causes', 18 *Tex. Tech L. Rev.* 1157, 1159 (1987) (emphasis omitted). Contrast this approach with that of Wendel; *see supra* Chapter 3.

As regards the second charge, it remains a fact that many people are already unable to secure any or adequate representation. Again, this is a function of economic factors. However, this also cuts in an ethical way as it means the problems of the poor are not only much less likely to be addressed and served by lawyers than those of the rich, but also that the very Standard Conception of lawyering will be more attuned to the interests of the haves, not the have-nots.[11] Of course, there is no reason to give either groups' interests priority in their access to the legal process. A resort to more openly ethical considerations would oblige the legal profession to confront those uncomfortable facts and oblige them to be more up-front in the bases for their choices in choosing clients. It is surely more in keeping with the ethical aspirations of the legal profession to act with integrity and honor if lawyers ensure that their services are distributed in line with ethical imperatives than by the economic status of their clientele.

None of this is to challenge the idea that everyone should be able to have a lawyer to represent them. But this is a collective responsibility of the legal profession; it does not fall upon the shoulders of each and every individual lawyer to meet that requirement. The central question for any lawyer will be to develop a plausible account of why he or she should be that lawyer. For example, there are lots of reasons tobacco companies should be able to obtain legal counsel (which they presently have very little problem doing), but there are few reasons it must be any particular lawyer. All lawyers must evaluate the justness of a cause and the rightfulness of its pursuers' intentions, but there will likely be different evaluations among lawyers in any particular case. However, in the unlikely situation of some lawyer being 'the last lawyer in town', the ethical appraisal may well come out differently; the overarching requirements of the system may well outweigh or trump the lawyer's personal convictions.[12]

Lawyers incur special ethical obligations to their clients, but this is not an unconditional or absolute commitment. While lawyers

[11] *See* Stephen Wexler, 'Practicing Law For Poor People', 79 *Yale L.J.* 1049 (1970).

[12] *See* Allan C. Hutchinson, *Legal Ethics and Professional Responsibility* 78–9 (2nd ed. 2006).

can withdraw their services only where there are compelling and justifiable reasons to do so, there are a few circumstances in which lawyers are obliged to withdraw from the case. In litigation, this occurs where clients want the lawyers to engage in prohibited conduct, such as knowingly deceiving the court or tribunal, taking malicious action, attempting to influence decisions or officials improperly and harassing witnesses. In such circumstances, after efforts to persuade clients of the impropriety of such conduct, lawyers must withdraw or seek the leave of the court to do so.[13] In non-litigious matters, lawyers have a similar obligation to withdraw where clients instruct them to act improperly, where they learn that a conflict of interest has occurred, or where they realize that they are no longer competent to handle the clients' matter.[14] In effecting withdrawal, lawyers must take all reasonable steps to protect the clients' interests, especially if the case is at a particularly crucial or vulnerable phase.

In many ways, a military-inspired account of legal ethics would build on this fragile foundation. It might be taken as insisting that lawyers can and should withdraw when changing circumstances begin to undermine the putative justness of the cause or impugn the clients' motivations; there is no initial accounting that gives the lawyer-client relationship or the clients' cause a once-and-for-all ethical imprimatur. Also, lawyers should be entitled to withdraw when evidence comes to light that the intentions of the clients are less honorable and rightful than first appeared to be the case. However, depending on how far the legal case or transaction has gone, there might well be countervailing factors that persuade lawyers to give clients more leeway and benefit of the doubt than would be the situation before the lawyer-client relationship was formalized. All this is a roundabout way of stating that lawyers must always be alert to the justness of the cause and the rightful intentions of clients throughout their representation.

[13] *See, for example*, *Model Rules of Prof'l Conduct* R. 1.16(a) (2002); *CBA Code of Prof'l Conduct* ch. IX cmt. 4, ch. XII cmt. 4 (2009); *SRA Code of Conduct* 2001 ch. 5 IB(5.5) (2013).

[14] *See, for example*, *Model Rules of Prof'l Conduct* R. 1.16(b) (2002); *CBA Code of Prof'l Conduct* ch. XII cmt. 5 (2009); *SRA Code of Conduct* 2011 chs. 1, 3 (2013).

It will, of course, be necessary to draw important distinctions between plaintiff clients and defendant clients in their 'just cause' rationale. This ethical rationale of 'just wars' obviously applies more easily and snugly to the representation of plaintiffs who usually set the ethical terms and legal parameters for litigation. Lawyers should be especially vigilant to be assured of the rightness of the plaintiffs' causes and the rightfulness of their intentions from the get-go. While lawyers for defendants will remain attentive to such matters, some allowance will need to be made for the fact that defendants have often not chosen to become litigants; they are not usually the aggressor or initiator of actions. Nevertheless, defendant lawyers will still need to be satisfied that their clients are defending a just position, that their intentions are appropriately honest, and that their intended tactics are fair. If not, it might well be incumbent on lawyers to decline to represent such defendants. In particular, there is no mandate to resort to unjust tactics simply because the other side has done so; ethical standards are not so easily abandoned or warped.

BEING COMPETENT

One of the more overlooked ethical responsibilities of lawyers is to act in a competent manner. All lawyers and regulatory bodies recognize the need for lawyers to be competent in what they do: they are expected to be competent to do what they undertake to do or be 'able to become competent without undue delay, risk or expense to the client'.[15] This is a continuing obligation that demands that they keep up to date. It is a contextual obligation in that the level of competence will vary with the subject matter being handled, the time made available and, therefore, the fees charged. Insofar as the expectation that lawyers will be capable of quality work affects the threshold issue of what cases and causes they take on, it has important ethical ramifications for whether they are engaged in pursuing just ends. In both military and legal contexts, incompetence undermines the fact that there might be otherwise just ends to pursue and just means to be deployed.

[15] *CBA Code of Prof'l Conduct* ch. II, cmt 3–5 (2009).

Unfortunately, the tendency among lawyers is to view the requirement of competence as more a legal requirement than a moral obligation. The law of torts imposes a duty upon lawyers to act as a 'reasonable lawyer'. It is not enough that a lawyer makes an error or a mistake; it must also be shown that it was the kind of error or mistake that reasonably competent lawyers would not make. While the appeal to the common professional customs in play will often be determinative, the courts have held that those customary practices must be demonstrably reasonable if lawyers are to escape liability.[16] Also, lawyers' duty to act competently is not confined to representing their clients; they can owe duties directly to third parties who might be foreseeably harmed by their actions (e.g., beneficiaries under a drafted will).[17]

However, lawyers also have a moral obligation to be competent that might be higher or lower in some situations than the prevailing standard of civil liability. For instance, it is incumbent on them to refuse involvement in cases for which they are untrained formally or by experience. While many lawyers do tend to specialize and thereby become more expert in their chosen field, there are many lawyers who take on files in areas in which they have little or no training and/or in which they soon realize that they are out of their professional depth. That said, most law societies are less than diligent in pursuing complaints of incompetence, let alone in disciplining lawyers over the quality of work performed. Although there have been recent initiatives to require evidence of continuing legal education before an annual license renewal, the practice and its policing are rudimentary and formal. Too often, lawyers maintain that they can get up to speed in short order and do a passable job for their client. Yet this is not an ethical way to go about lawyering.

An exacting standard of professional ethics demands that lawyers do more than offer a basic level of competence and service. Although the issue of competence is often viewed through the lens

[16] *See*, for example, *Dorion v. Roberge*, [1991] 1 S.C.R. 374.

[17] *See Central & Eastern Trust Co. v. Rafuse*, [1986] 2 S.C.R. 147; *White v. Jones*, [1995] 2 A.C. 207 (H.L.); and *Morales v. Field, DeGoff, Huppert & MacGowan*, 160 Cal. Rptr.239 (Ct. App. 1980).

of individual cases, there is an ethical component to the evaluation of lawyers' overall work. For instance, while there well may be egregious examples of lawyers who take cases for which they have no training and experience or in which they perform carelessly and shoddily, there is also the very real problem of lawyers who may well be skilled and talented, but who simply take on too many files and too many clients. In these situations, lawyers' time and attention are stretched too thinly. Although they manage to do a passable job, they do not give clients the care and focus that they are capable of doing or that the files deserve. This is a mode of lawyering that may or may not amount to incompetence, but it surely is an ethical failing. Over time, this will result in some clients and causes failing to achieve the kind of outcomes that might be expected or warranted. What might have begun as a just and winnable campaign is destined to end in failure and perhaps injustice.

The upshot of such a cavalier or neglectful attitude to the important issue of professional competence is that, no matter how just the ends, a cause cannot be pursued ethically by lawyers who are not up to the task. In military terms, it is not only that an otherwise just war will be poorly and harmfully waged by untrained recruits, but also that the justness of any campaign will be tainted and perhaps undermined by proceeding with incompetent troops: incompetence will contribute to the waging of a war that will have reduced chances of success. In lawyering terms, it will mean that not only is the client being ill served by a less than fully competent lawyer, but that the attainment of just causes will be seriously and substantially compromised. If there is to be an exacting standard of ethical behavior imposed on lawyers, then it will recommend that lawyers must be scrupulous in only offering their services when they are fully able to perform the tasks involved with high and dependable professional quality.

GOING TO COURT

A particular and practical implication of a reliance on military ethics is that lawyers might have to become more litigation-shy. There presently exist directives not to commence litigation where, for instance, the motivation is 'malicious' or the main purpose is 'to embarrass, delay, or burden a third person'.[18] While these are not trivial constraints on lawyers' behavior, they do not require lawyers to engage in any serious assessment of the costs and benefits of litigation as regards the overall effect on all parties, chances of success, proportionality and so forth. From an ethical standpoint, more is required to validate lawyers' and clients' actions as 'rightful' than them simply not being malicious or ill-intended. The need for a just cause is an affirmative responsibility that asks much more than that lawyers refrain from acting in the worst cases and for the worst reasons.

Indeed, the requirement of 'proportionality' places clear restrictions on when and even if litigation should be commenced. It will be necessary for lawyers to take serious stock of the good that is to be achieved by litigation and to offset it against the inevitable harm that is to be done. In perhaps its most expansive mode, this assessment will need to include the interests of all parties and perhaps non-parties, enemy and ally alike, to the legal action; it will not be an insular or limited examination that only calibrates the client's interests. Unless this balancing comes out clearly in determining that the benefits/good are greater than or reasonably proportional to the costs/evil, only then will it be acceptable to advise a client to initiate litigation. While clients are free to obtain counsel that will take a less assiduous stance, this does not mean that all lawyers should set aside or dilute their moral standards and proceed to litigate. The fact that some lawyers might take a different and less rigorous approach is not a license for other lawyers to forego their own ethical analysis and responsibility. A moral dialogue between lawyer and client is to be encouraged.

Moreover, even if such a positive proportionality is forthcoming, the demand that litigation be a 'last resort' and have a 'reasonable chance of success' will impose further constraints on lawyers' willingness to launch litigation. As some professional rules are now beginning to demand, lawyers must engage in settlement talks and other alternative dispute resolution efforts before resorting to formal litigation; this must be done in good faith and with an eye to

[18] *See, for example*, *Model Rules of Prof'l Conduct* R. 4.4(a) (2002) and *CBA Code of Prof'l Conduct* ch. IX, 2(a) (2009).

reaching a fair and just resolution of the case.[19] Again, the intentions of the client must be rightful and honest; there is no ethical brief for going through the motions in settlement talks or court-mandated mediation before commencing the already decided on strategy of litigation. Similarly, lawyers must be persuaded that, because of the inevitable toll that litigation will take on all concerned, there is some genuine chance of litigation bringing about a successful and beneficial resolution to matters. The reliance on disproportionate measures should be anathema to the ethical lawyer.

Of course, most jurisdictions do place a formal restraint on lawyers' decision to commence litigation. For instance, Rule 11(b), (2) of the U.S. Federal Rules of Civil Procedure obliges lawyers to certify that any legal claims made in their pleadings are, among other things, 'warranted by existing law or by a non-frivolous argument for extending, modifying, or reversing existing law or for establishing new law... after an inquiry reasonable under the circumstances'.[20] While there is a strong case to be made for including such a constraint in any series of ethical injunctions, it is wildly optimistic to make it the almost exclusive benchmark by which to control and discipline lawyers. Again, while these rule-based strictures operate as a check on the more flagrant abuses of initiating litigation in oppressive circumstances and for the wrong reasons, they represent a minimal baseline, not an ethical ceiling. A legal professional sensibility informed by military ethics would require a much more subtle and demanding standard of analysis before litigation was commenced.

In the criminal law context, these self-policed ethical preconditions might recommend that prosecutors invoke a conscious analysis of proportionality when deciding whether to issue a grand jury subpoena or charge, seek a search warrant or take any other investigative step. Such analyses would need to account for the costs not

[19] *See, for example, Model Rules of Prof'l Conduct* R. 2.1 cmt. para. 5 (2002); *CBA Code of Prof'l Conduct* ch. III cmt. 6, ch. IX cmt. 8 (2009); *SRA Code of Conduct* 2011 ch. 1 (2013).

[20] Until amended in 1993, 'non-frivolous argument' used to read 'a good faith argument'. *See Nemeroff v. Abelson*, 620 F. 2d 339 (2d Cir. 1980) and *Kinee v. Abraham Lincoln Fed. Saving & Loan Assoc.*, 365 F. Supp. 975 (E.D.Pa. 1973). *See infra*, ch.3.

only to the government, but also to the targets of such measures and other affected third parties.[21] Furthermore, prosecutors might well consider not only monetary costs, but also significant intangible costs such as privacy intrusions, emotional stress and social stigma. In short, they should balance those costs against factors such as the gravity of the offense, the likely benefit from the proposed investigative step and whether any less costly (including less intrusive) steps might suffice. An ethical mandate would emphasize the need for such analyses, even if they would likely be impressionistic and far from uniform in occurrence and application.

As regards civil litigation, the calculations might play out slightly differently. Because it will often be the case that financial or economic considerations will be more central, it will be important for lawyers to be more wide-ranging in their assessment of proportionality. It will not be sufficient for lawyers to ensure that the time and expense invested in litigation on behalf of their clients is proportionate to the issues and interests at stake for their clients. Again, an ethical lawyer might be required to look at the broader institutional and social costs that litigation imposes on parties and non-parties alike in terms of the monetary value, complexity and social importance of the dispute. As one astute judge has noted, 'proportional litigation is pivotal to ensuring true access to justice.'[22] And this should be as much an ethical concern of the legal profession as the ultimate success of individual clients' cases.

CONCLUSION

Accordingly, an important implication for legal ethics of taking a leaf out of the military ethicist's book is that lawyers would need to give more serious attention to their choice of clients and the causes that they represent. It would not be sufficient to take the traditional and recommended hands-off neutral position on whom they represent and why they do so. However, in taking more personal

[21] Rory K. Little, Symposium, 'Proportionality as an Ethical Precept for Prosecutors in Their Investigative Role', 68 *Fordham L. Rev.* 723 (2000).

[22] Warren K. Winkler, 'Professionalism and Proportionality', 27 *Advocate's J.* 6 (2009).

responsibility for the clients served and the causes pursued, lawyers will not be expected only to take clients and causes that align directly and closely with their own substantive values. As always, lawyers-as-warriors are professionals and will simply need to be satisfied with the bona fides of their clients' intentions and goals. This offers a wide range of possibilities to both lawyers and clients. That said, having examined the traditional requirements of a just war, I will now turn to the implications of the just war theory for the methods and tactics used to prosecute such a just war.

7

Fighting Fair

The debate within military and legal ethics about the nature and limits of the professional means used to achieve appropriate and just ends is part of a larger and more expansive moral debate around 'fair play'. The primary quandary is over both whether the ends can ever justify the means and whether different ends warrant different means: If the end is so warranted and so just can it sanction the use of any means to achieve it? Or does the resort to unjust and extreme means go so far as to negate or invalidate the previous justness of the ends sought? These are pertinent and perennial challenges for both military officers and professional lawyers. Most would agree that, even if the ends to be pursued were entirely just and warranted, this does not give people carte blanche to achieve those ends by whatever means possible. This would be less an ethical stance and more an abandonment of one.

ENDS AND MEANS

The basic thrust of military ethics is that any and all violence in war must be justified: it counsels a minimalist approach. No matter how just or worthy the cause undertaken, the prosecution of a just war demands that only just methods be used – the moral defensibility of the ends do not justify the resort to any possible means to achieve them. Moreover, the ethical focus is on both the *why* and the *how* of military action.[1] Intentions and consequences must be evaluated

[1] *See* Peter Temes, *The Just War* (2003); *Just War in Comparative Perspective* (Paul Robinson ed., 2003); Brian Orend, *The Morality of War* (2006).

together. Bad motives can taint what would otherwise be a justified consequence. Indeed, on a more general scale, if warring parties engage in unjust means, this can seriously compromise the justness of the war being waged. Accordingly, violence that is not militarily necessary violates *jus in bello*, but not all violence deemed militarily necessary is morally permissible.

While there is much heated and unresolved debate around the main indicia for just means, it is generally conceded that, in order to pass the test of what is to count as just means, any violent or unlawful conduct within a just war must meet twin and mutually reinforcing criteria of assessment:

(1) **A Discriminate Deployment of Force** – Just war conduct should be governed by the principle of distinction. The acts of war should be directed toward enemy combatants, and not toward noncombatants or civilians caught in circumstances they did not create. The prohibited acts include bombing civilian residential areas that include no military target and committing acts of terrorism or reprisal against ordinary civilians; and

(2) **A Proportionate Balance Between Action Taken and Objective to Be Achieved** – Just war conduct should be governed by a principle of proportionality whereby action cannot be launched in the knowledge that the harm caused would be clearly excessive in relation to the concrete and direct military advantage anticipated: there must be proportionality in the chosen method and desired objective. In line with this, there are several accepted components of this responsibility:
- Selection and use of weapons;
- No 'over-killing';
- Prevention of unnecessary suffering and destruction;
- Selection of military targets;
- Avoidance of civilian targets; and
- Invalidity of retaliatory strikes.

As with the conditions for entering a just war, the criteria for 'just means' do not provide or ensure tidy or unambiguous answers to difficult questions about what amounts to proper and appropriate conduct in waging a just war. The overriding ethical concern is to keep the relative means used within reasonable and realistic parameters. However, while respect for these considerations will place definite restrictions on the military strategies pursued and tactics adopted, there is still considerable room for maneuver; the freedom of military commanders is tightly constrained, but far from expunged. Consequently, the practical conduct of war rests in the hands of individual military officers who bear responsibility for day-to-day activity and operations.[2] As such, military ethics does not act as a definitive manual for conducting a just war, but as a set of discursive resources to frame reflection and orient decision making.

There are, of course, many implications to be drawn from the tradition and directives of *ius in bello* for developing a greater richness and depth in discussions about what counts as ethical means of lawyering. Three particular insights are evident. The first is that the prevailing view that lawyers have few, if any, responsibilities to opposing and/or third parties is clearly unsustainable: lawyers would need to ensure that their work for their clients impaired the rights and interests of others as little as possible.[3] Second, lawyers would be required to measure their maneuvers in light of the opposing parties' motivations and resources; there would have to be a greater recognition that there was often a large and important inequality between parties, especially in the case of unrepresented litigants. Third, it might be important to explore the need to develop a doctrine of 'superior orders' in assessing the differential duties of junior and senior lawyers in the hierarchical contexts of large law firms.[4] However, before pursuing these discrete topics, it is instructive to reflect more generally on the whole idea and practice of 'fighting fair' and its general ethical imperatives in the professional context of lawyers.

[2] Martin L. Cook, *The Moral Warrior* 32 (2004).

[3] Richard J. Arneson, 'Just Warfare Theory and Noncombatant Immunity', NN *Cornell Int'l L.J.* 101 (2007).

[4] Andrew M. Perlman, 'Unethical Obedience by Subordinate Attorneys: Lessons from Social Psychology', 36 *Hofstra L. Rev.* 451 (2007).

FIGHTING FAIR

The basic ethical tension in play in evaluating the justness and appropriateness of means used is between consequentialist and deontological views. The former insists that it is sometimes necessary to resort to immoral means to achieve significant goals or ends; the moral worthiness of any action is ultimately determined by the outcome or consequences of that action. In its more stark Machiavellian form, this is less a morality and more an excuse for one.[5] The latter view maintains that the ends can never justify the means and that the reliance on immoral means is fatal to any evaluation of the overall goal or conduct. Again, in its more stark Kantian mode, this is an unrealistic guide to moral conduct as it cautions against even the smallest moral infraction to achieve a pressing moral end (e.g., lying to save another's life).[6] Accordingly, any scheme of professional ethics must combine some elements of each.

Of course, as the ethics of warfare suggests, any evaluation of moral worthiness must be contextual and pragmatic; there is no one fixed measure of whether any particular means is justifiable in the abstract. For instance, while killing others may generally be treated as immoral, it can be justified in certain settings and circumstances depending on the ends to be achieved and the alternatives available. That said, it must surely be the case that a professional morality must recognize that the end does not always justify the means and that sometimes, if not always, there are definite limits on the means used to pursue ones' goals. Consequently, while 'proportionality' is the governing standard, some means are so loathsome and egregious (e.g., chemical warfare) that they are never considered acceptable or justifiable whatever the overall justness of the ends sought. Indeed, the unjustness of the means might well compromise what are otherwise entirely just ends (e.g., the use of nuclear weapons).

This ethical dilemma is neatly captured in the less fraught and more modest setting of sporting contests. 'Fair play' refers to all participants having an equitable chance to pursue victory and in

[5] Niccolò Machiavelli, *The Prince* (Harvey C. Mansfield trans., 2nd ed. 1998) (1532).

[6] Immanuel Kant, *Groundwork for the Metaphysics of Morals* (1785).

acting toward others in an honest, straightforward and dignified manner even when others do not play fairly. An individual or team is believed to have 'played fairly' when their actions exhibit virtues such as fairness, self-control, courage, respect and persistence. Of course, there is no reason to assume that two people who act with integrity will agree on what is right and wrong or on a common course of action. Good faith cannot in itself tell people what to do in situations of uncertainty and doubt; it can only give them the courage to act on their own convictions in a way that takes seriously the responsibility to act fairly.[7] Accordingly, 'fair play' can be thought of as acting in line not only with the prevailing rules, but also within the spirit of the enterprise in which one is engaged.

Perhaps surprisingly, the writings of the existential French writer Albert Camus evoke this moral tension between means and ends in the sporting context – the desires to play to win and to play fair. He saw that his football (or soccer) experience had placed front and center the need to make the 'difficult compromise' between 'playing sportingly' and 'playing strongly'. For him, it was important – and went to the very idea of what it meant to be 'a man' – to recognize that winning was not everything and that how you played the game was as important; there is a price of victory that is too high in the continuing game of life. Camus saw that it is only when you know what it means to *play the game* and live by its injunctions that people can truly be treated as fully human and worthy of other's admiration and respect.[8]

This approach offers much-needed insight and illumination to the discussion of both military and legal ethics. In particular, it recommends that the distinction between legitimate and illegitimate behavior is not a bright line, but a spectrum of options and choices. The ideal of 'natural' or 'fair play' is itself part of the argumentative contest over what it means to *play the game*.[9] It is not possible to withdraw to some grounded position outside the contested area to

[7] S. Carter, *Integrity* 7 (1996). *See also* Martin Benjamin, *Splitting the Difference* (1990); Sissela Bok, *Lying* (1978); Lynn McFall, 'Integrity', 98 *Ethics* 5 (1987).

[8] *See* Albert Camus, 'The Wager of Our Generation', in *Resistance, Rebellion and Death* 242 (Justine O'Brien trans., 1960).

[9] *See* Allan C. Hutchinson, *It's All in the Game: A Non-foundationalist Account of Law and Adjudication* (2000).

validate or vouchsafe objective standards for evaluation or criticism: there is no escape from the responsibility of choosing among competing values. As with all such discussions, whether in sport, war or law, the context and timing of the argumentative contest will influence the problem and its resolution – what counts as cheating is no less (or more) contingent than what counts as good play. There are situations in which adherence to the so-called letter of the rules can be taken to violate the spirit of the game as much as deviate from them.

As regards legal ethics, this tension between playing to win and playing fairly runs deep within both the professional rules and the general academic commentary on professional responsibility. At its most uncompromising, there is a view that is particularly evident in criminal law – that lawyers not only can, but should use all available and legal means at their disposal to serve their clients by playing to win (i.e., to seek acquittals).[10] This is defended as the very definition of zealous and partisan advocacy; there is no room for professional or personal moral qualms in pursuing the clients' moral and justified ends. Of course, there are others who point out that this is no ethics at all: the domain of the ethical is abandoned entirely and reduced to the mandate of not breaking the law. In contrast, there is an approach that urges lawyers to place playing fairly above all other considerations; winning a particular trial or motion is thought a distinctly secondary ambition compared to the need to preserve professional reputation and moral esteem by playing fairly and thereby promoting the *justice* system generally.[11] Whereas the former tends to put clients' interests ahead of all others, the latter might well place the profession's and the system's interests ahead of all others. Neither seems a particularly worthy goal on its own exclusive terms.

In the next few sections, I show how this tension between playing to win and playing fairly is manifested in specific instances of legal professional ethics – they can be grouped together under the responsibility, if any, owed to the interests of non-clients. The practice and theory of professional lawyering has little to say or advise

[10] Charles Curtis, 'The Ethics of Advocacy', 4 *Stan. L. Rev.* 3, 5 (1951).

[11] William Simon, *The Practice of Justice* (1998).

on these important and thorny problems. However, the principles and resources of military ethics (i.e., discrimination and proportionality) can offer assistance in working through this legal challenge in a more sophisticated and reflective manner; they can shine a more nuanced light on the intricacies and implications of how the interests of adversaries, represented or not, and third parties might be understood and taken into account. It helps to turn the monochrome world of legal ethics into a better and more technicolor universe of professional responsibility.

COLLATERAL DAMAGE

An abiding principle of military ethics is that of 'civilian immunity' (or 'discrimination'). This concept was first developed in codes and customs of chivalry in the Middle Ages. Because conflicts were between princes rather than between societies at large, there was little reason to attack ordinary people and those who did were judged to be acting dishonorably. At its most general, this principle demands that all steps must be taken to eliminate or, at least, reduce intentional harm to those who are not actively or 'currently engaged in the business of war'.[12] However, this idea is based on two important, but contested distinctions: Who is and is not involved in 'the business of war'? And what counts as 'intentional harm'? Whereas the first speaks to the elusive contrast between combatants and civilians, the second raises the controversial issue of so-called collateral damage.

Although there is widespread agreement that civilians should be immune from the direct effects of war, there is substantial disagreement on who exactly is to be granted the status of a civilian or noncombatant. Apart from the obvious case of active military personnel, it is not self-evident who else is engaged in the business of war so as to make them fair targets for military action. Many people are indirectly involved in the business of war by way of providing services to military personnel, especially those making or transporting munitions and supplies. However, it is clear that

[12] Michael Walzer, *Just and Unjust Wars: A Moral Argument with Historical Illustrations* 43 (3rd ed. 2000).

children and the elderly are almost always to be seen as civilians for immunity purposes. Also, military personnel who have surrendered or are incapacitated are to be treated as noncombatants and, thereby, receive appropriate immunity and protection.[13]

After negotiating the combatant-civilian challenge, the second issue that has occupied military ethicists is the extent of immunity accorded to those designated as noncombatants. Are there circumstances in which engaging in military action that has significant potential for serious and extensive harm to civilians can ever be justified? An important distinction has been drawn between intentional and accidental harm caused to civilian populations. While the direct targeting of noncombatants is prohibited, it is considered acceptable for there to be some harm or injury as a consequence of justified attacks on combatants. Accordingly, 'collateral damage' is permissible provided that the intended military action is serving a compelling goal, that no alternative safer method of action is available, and that steps are taken to minimize all incidental harm. Of course, these conditions are far from easy to define or put into precise operational effect. For instance, while the development of more sophisticated weaponry has arguably enabled more focused military action, it is a matter of informed and good faith judgment as to how and when such criteria can be weighed and balanced (e.g., the use of drone planes).[14]

[13] John Coverdale, 'An Introduction to the Just War Tradition', 16 *Pace Int' L. Rev.* 221 at 264–7 (2004) and Jeffrie G. Murphy, 'The Killing of the Innocent', in *War, Morality, and the Military Profession* 341, 350 (Malham M. Wakin ed., 2d. ed. 1986). There is also guidance in international law on this matter. Article 51 of Protocol I provides that 'the civilian population as such, as well as individual civilians, shall not be the object of attack.' *See* Protocol I, June 1977, additional to the Geneva Conventions of 1949. Also, the third Geneva Convention of 1949 sets forth categories of legitimate combatants. *See* Geneva Convention Relative to the Treatment of Prisoners of War art. 4A, Aug. 12, 1949, 6 U.S.T. 3316, 75 U.N.T.S. 135.

[14] A case in point is the use of saturation bombing, which often claims massive civilian casualties (e.g., the destruction of Hiroshima and Dresden). While many consider such tactics unacceptable and on a par with chemical warfare, others contend that such harm must be weighed against the future lives saved by such drastic and often war-ending tactics. *See* Coverdale, *supra*, note 13. Also, there is an important debate about the distinction between soldiers and terrorists. For example, Michael Ignatieff argues that it is 'the definition of terror to obliterate that distinction, to attack civilians and make this the very purpose of the action'. *See* Michael Ignatieff, 'Ethics and the New War', 2 *Canadian Mil. J.* 5 (Winter 2001).

It will be appreciated that these matters of military ethics – the combatant/civilian distinction and the avoidance of collateral damage – have suggestive and useful merit in familiar debates within legal ethics. For instance, the question of 'who is the client?' is of paramount importance in determining lawyers' duties, even if the resulting duties that its resolution gives rise to are not absolute or exclusive. Although it will be easy to ascertain the identity of the client in many situations, it can quickly and frequently become more problematic. The landscape of professional responsibility has become populated by all sorts of characters and caricatures, including current clients, former clients, future clients, quasi-clients, organizational clients, group clients and non-clients. It is a veritable *dramatis personae* who morph in and out of their different identities and occasionally hold more than one personality across time or at one time. Consequently, in thinking about legal ethics and responsibilities, it is prudent to treat the lawyer-client relationship as a shifting and multidimensional connection that gives rise to correspondingly changing obligations.

As with military ethics, this shifting terrain has important ramifications for the nature and limits of lawyers' duties toward clients and others. The duties owed toward clients will often take priority, but they are not absolute or all-consuming. While it is clear that lawyers must and should put their clients' interests first, this obligation does not mean that they should not or need not take into account the interests of others when they are acting for clients. The duty to be a zealous partisan in the pursuit of clients' interests involves the prioritizing of clients' interests, not the obliteration of everyone else's: it simply means that lawyers can give their clients' interests more weight on the scales than those of others. Other interests still count, but for less.

Consequently, while it is essential to identify who is and who is not a client as the triggering event for the important legal and ethical responsibilities of zealous advocacy (i.e., confidentiality, loyalty and the like), it is also important to emphasize that lawyers' legal and ethical obligations might not and should not start and finish with clients. Definite and variable responsibilities to others can be factored into the ethical equation when plotting and initiating appropriate professional behavior. Although often overlooked and ignored, there are many duties that lawyers might have that are independent of their relationship with clients. Like all professionals, lawyers owe an extensive series of professional duties to the legal process at large (e.g., not to mislead courts) and to their professional communities and colleagues (e.g., to uphold the Rule of Law and not to impose unreasonable conditions on colleagues).[15] These legal obligations and moral responsibilities provide a backdrop against which the central relationship between lawyers and clients can be better understood and grasped. So understood, the ethical responsibilities of lawyers become much more nuanced and much more contestable.

Apart from any specific contractual obligations that lawyers assume in their commercial dealings with others, there are several tortious and equitable duties that lawyers might owe people and organizations at large. These are in addition to a number of moral responsibilities that lawyers assume as qualified legal professionals. In particular, the notion of avoiding collateral damage has considerable purchase in thinking about the treatment of persons and organizations that are not clients. For instance, like accountants and financial advisers, lawyers can owe a duty of care to persons who rely on lawyers' advice to their detriment. This is most apparent in regard to wills and estates, but can also extend to other areas, such as contract.[16] Accordingly, the need to avoid collateral damage is already a set, if neglected feature of the lawyering terrain.

Taking non-clients' interests into account is a step beyond simply owing general duties to non-clients. As a general rule, lawyers can owe a duty to a third party (even if that party is represented) and courts have been prepared to go as far as imposing a fiduciary duty on lawyers to non-clients in some situations. For example, in a real estate transaction, it was held that a purchaser's lawyer could owe a fiduciary duty to the vendors because they were unrepresented and the lawyer knew or ought to have known that the elderly and

[15] *See, for example, Model Rules of Prof'l Conduct* pmbl. (2002); *CBA Code of Prof'l Conduct* ch. 1 (2009); *SRA Code of Conduct* 2011 Principles (2013).

[16] *See White v. Jones*, [1995] 1 AC 691 (H.L.); *Hill v. Van Erp* (1997), 142 ALR 687 (Austl. H.C.); *Goodman v. Kennedy*, 18 Cal. 3d 335, 134 Cal. Rptr. 375 (1976); and *Whittingham v. Crease & Co.* (1978), 88 DLR (3d) 353 (Can. B.C. S.C.).

unrepresented vendors were or might be relying on him to protect their interests. Expressly stating that this decision was not based on the existence of an implied retainer, the judge stated that 'though fiduciary responsibilities normally arise from an existing contractual relationship of solicitor and client, the contractual tie is not essential.'[17]

But there has been understandable reluctance to impose such a duty if the third party is adverse in interest as this will dilute and hamper the lawyers' duties to their own clients.[18] This is where the concept of avoiding collateral damage becomes useful: it adds much needed flesh to the skeletal idea that lawyers should treat all persons 'involved in the legal process with courtesy and respect'.[19] It might be that, when allied with a requirement of proportionality, such considerations will place genuine and concrete limitations on what lawyers can do for their clients. This will be less of an independent duty, but more of a side-constraint on the duty owed to one's clients or the system at large.

PROPORTIONALITY

In the same way that there is a proportionality dimension to entering a just war, there is also a requirement that the methods and tactics for waging war must respect and instantiate proportionality. In short, there must be a proportionate balance between any action taken and the military objective; it is unjustified to embark on an initiative that will cause more harm than any likely advantage.

[17] *See Tracy v. Atkins* (1977), 83 D.L.R. (3d) 46, para. 27 (Can. B.C. S.C.). This decision was upheld on the narrow ground of negligence in *Tracy v. Atkins* (1997), 195 D.L.R. (3d) 632 (Can. B.C. C.A.). Again, a lender's solicitor will have a fiduciary duty to a borrower's spouse to ensure that he or she receives independent legal advice where that person is unrepresented and unfamiliar with legal matters. *See Shoppers Trust Co. v. Dynamic Homes Ltd.* (1992), 96 D.L.R. (4th) 267 (Can. Ont. GenDiv); *Morales v. Field, DeGoff, Huppert & MacGowan*, 99 Cal. App. 3d 307 (1979); *Dean v. Allin & Watts* [2001] EWCA (Civ) 758 (Eng.).

[18] *See Nelles v. Ontario*, [1989] 2 S.C.R. 170 (Can.); *Winters v. Schulman*, 977 P.2d 1218 (Utah Ct. App. 1999). *Gran Gelato Ltd. v Richcliff (Group) Ltd.* [1992] Ch. 560; [1992] 2 W.L.R. 867 (Eng.).

[19] *Model Rules of Prof'l Conduct* R. 1.3 cmt. para. 1 (2002). *See also CBA Code of Prof'l Conduct* ch. IX cmt. 15 (2009); *SRA Code of Conduct* 2011 Principles (2013).

Method and goal must correlate in a fitting and countervailing way. This proportionality component operates in close tandem with the 'civilian immunity' criterion. While this principle concedes that it is not always practical to distinguish between combatants and non-combatants, proportionality demands that any collateral damage be as inadvertent and as minimal as possible in the circumstances. Destruction and harm beyond what is necessary to achieve a military objective is ethically condemned and to be avoided. However, to achieve a military objective through the least destructive means possible (and thereby reduce the amount of collateral damage), the military must sometimes assume increased personal risk. This trade-off makes for difficult choices. Needless to say, the precise contours of proportionality are far from settled or fixed.

In modern warfare, it is presumed that certain tactics and weapons are almost always considered disproportionate. These include biological, chemical or nuclear weapons, mass rape and ethnic cleansing that wreak havoc of enormous proportions. Also, there is wide consensus that certain locations cannot be the primary targets of military offensives (e.g., schools, hospitals and places of worship) because they are likely to contain large civilian gatherings and populations. However, there is less consensus on whether so-called open targets, such as towns and villages, are legitimate locations for military aggression. Finally, there is no warrant for one side to treat the unjust actions of its enemies as a justification for engaging in similar unjust actions. Proportionality only operates within the realm of just actions; revenge is always a dish best not served at all.

The importance in the legal professional setting of these proportional limits to just means is general, but insightful. There are certain actions lawyers might be tempted to take that are considered beyond the ethical pale in almost all circumstances; they are considered the chemical weapons of legal ethics. The more obvious ones include fabricating documents, acting contradictory to clients' instructions and counseling criminal behavior. However, some actions are frowned upon by many, but not by all; these include not correcting false information and understandings, facilitating the presentation of misleading evidence and rigidly insisting on strict deadlines. However, the real benefit of using military ethics as a filter through which to view legal professional responsibility is that it demands that lawyers take non-clients into direct account when advancing the interests and wishes of their clients in a proportionate way.

In line with the prohibition of not initiating frivolous or maliciously motivated litigation, lawyers should not advance just litigation by tactics and arguments that are themselves vexatious and not merit-based.[20] Lawyers are under an obligation to resist and temper, not cultivate and indulge the understandable temptation of some clients to act badly against adversaries. As such, lawyers must be diligent in ensuring that they do not become the dupes of their clients and that they act with good faith generally. In particular, they should refrain from taking advantage of slips or oversights by other parties that do not go to the real merits of the dispute or transaction and from adopting tactics that will merely delay or harass the other side. As one military code puts it, 'belligerents ... conduct hostilities with regard for the principles of humanity and chivalry.'[21] This, of course, has its more focused analogue for lawyers in the need not to bring the administration of justice and the legal profession into disrepute.

A discrete example of proportionality in context is the lot assumed by lawyers involved in criminal prosecutions. Theirs is not the one-sided and blinkered approach the standard model of ethical lawyering recommends; a greater degree of dispassionateness and evenhandedness is encouraged.[22] From a prosecuting lawyer's viewpoint, the just end in question is not a conviction, but rather the fair administration of justice. Although it is not the prosecuting lawyers' job to do the defense lawyers' job for them or to work for an accused's acquittal, it is their responsibility to ensure that convictions are only achieved as a matter of substantive and procedural justice. This stands in sharp contrast to the role and responsibility of criminal defense lawyers whose role is to work robustly toward the acquittal of the accused client.[23]

[20] *See Model Rules of Prof'l Conduct* R. 3.1 (2002); *CBA Code of Prof'l Conduct* ch. IX cmt. 7 (2009); *SRA Code of Conduct Rule* 11.05(a), (c)-(d (2013). *See also supra* Chapter 6.

[21] U.S. Army, *Law of Land Warfare*, Ch. 1, s.1(3) (1956).

[22] *See Model Rules of Prof'l Conduct* R. 3.8 (2002); *CBA Code of Prof'l Conduct* ch. IX cmt. 9 (2009); *SRA Code of Conduct* R. 11, guid. 18(b) (2013).

[23] *See supra* Chapter 4.

Drawing on military officers' responsibility to minimize collateral damage, it is reasonable to recommend that there is also little or no reason for lawyers to facilitate their clients' efforts to harm another's interests deliberately. This is especially so if such actions would not substantially improve the situation of their own clients: doing harm for its own sake should be anathema to any professional. Consequently, a strong case can be made for requiring lawyers to ensure that, in robustly advancing their clients' interests, they effect a proportionate balance between the good to be attained by their client and the harm to be suffered by others, including both the opposing parties and third parties generally. While lawyers are not obliged to assist adversaries or be solicitous toward others' interests that are directly antagonistic to their clients' own interests, they can be reasonably asked to reduce any incidental harm to others and not to harm others for the sake of it. Such restraint will not necessarily jeopardize lawyers' primary obligation to be decidely partisan in performing their professional duties. Moreover, this approach might actually enhance the ethical role and decision making of lawyers generally in advancing the public interest.[24]

Traditionalists might argue that without single-minded and uncluttered attention to clients' interests, lawyers might find themselves co-opted into the very system that the best traditions of the legal profession are devoted to challenging. It can be argued that the fact that lawyers' duties to their clients can be overridden by their higher obligation to the courts, the public or the profession generally will compromise their devotion to their clients' interests; the individual's quest for justice can be considered to be sacrificed to professional solidarity or established interests. This argument has some appeal if (and only if) lawyers are willing to take responsibility for the clients they represent and the tactics they employ.[25] Many lawyers are reluctantly drawn to adopting intimidating or inconveniencing tactics on the basis that they will not be competitive enough and will not be able to defend their client successfully against those who persist in using such tactics. Such a vicious cycle

[24] *See Model Rules of Prof'l Conduct* R. 4.4 (2002); *CBA Code of Prof'l Conduct* ch. IX cmt. 2. (2009); *SRA Code of Conduct* 2011 ch. 11(2013).

[25] *See supra* Chapter 6.

of justification is to be resisted and rejected. Otherwise, any claim to ethical propriety is hollow and will only serve to clothe the mundane defense of the status quo with the dubious vestments of undeserved legitimacy.

THE ADVERSARIAL DILEMMA

A particular aspect of this general challenge for the ethical lawyer is how to deal with and toward the other side(s) in any dispute. For some, the traditional view of the Standard Conception of ethical lawyering is built on the need to 'treat outsiders as if they were barbarians and enemies', there are considered to be 'situations in which a lawyer may be duty bound to lie for his client'.[26] The basic logic behind this uncompromising stand is that the role of lawyers is to act as champions for their clients, not as their moral consciences. As part of viewing your adversary in such negative terms, it becomes the prime ethical mandate of litigating lawyers to 'do what you can to help friend and harm enemy, as long as you stay within the law'.[27] This injunction to 'do harm' is an unduly harsh and unhelpful interpretation of even the Standard Conception of lawyering. It is especially troublesome and downright unethical when under a reconceived vision of the lawyer as an honorable warrior. Although an opponent is there to be beaten in both military action and litigation, it does not mean that they are to be harmed for the sake of it or humiliiated. Warriors respect their enemies, not demonize or demean them.

In contrast, an honorable lawyer should strenuously resist any impulse or clients' direction to adopt a consistently bellicose or thoroughly hostile stance toward all others, including a direct opposing party. At a minimum, this restraint is part of the overall obligation to treat opposing parties and their counsel with courtesy and civility; war or litigation is not an occasion when such qualities of decency need to be thrown entirely out the window. That said, a direct adversary can be treated differently than others. However, exactly what that entails is far from clear. Again, the role and responsibilities of criminal defense lawyers seem to be the

[26] Curtis, *supra* note 10, at 5.
[27] *Id.* at 7.

exception that proves the general rule. Apart from retaining a civil and professional manner in dealing with the prosecution, such lawyers are entitled and expected to do all that they can to be vigorous and uncompromising in achieving an acquittal for their clients. But this approach need not and likely should not be carried over into other matters and areas of law.

In noncriminal matters, this expectation of a less hostile attitude toward the opposing party can most easily be explained and justified by reference to some of the more general duties that lawyers already owe to the legal process and administration of justice at large.[28] In particular, this way of approaching the adversarial dilemma tends to sidestep the difficult issue of how to balance the apparent competing and conflicting responsibilities by lawyers to their clients and opposing parties. Under such general duties, it is required of lawyers that they act honorably and with integrity to all persons with which they come in contact; this includes opposing parties and their lawyers. For instance, they must take care not to resort to offensive tactics and not to take advantage of slips or irregularities. In so doing, lawyers will be able to ensure that the interests of their clients are appropriately balanced against the overall demands of the system within which lawyers work. Most significantly, it will act as a suitable corrective to the win-at-all-costs mentality that any honorable lawyer or warrior ought to reject.

These already challenging matters – Are there any duties or responsibilities owed to opposing parties? What are they? And what are their limits? – are made doubly difficult if the opposing parties do not have the assistance of a lawyer. These so-called self-represented litigants are becoming increasingly common in court proceedings. While there are a whole host of reasons for this disturbing trend, it is estimated that about 40 percent of all litigants are self-represented; this can rise to close to 80 percent in family law matters.[29] One of the many challenges that this phenomenon poses to traditional thinking on legal ethics is the effect on the accepted behavior of

[28] *See, for example*, *Model Rules of Prof'l Conduct* R. 3.1 (2002); *CBA Code of Prof'l Conduct* ch. IX, *Comm.* 7 (2009); *SRA Code of Conduct* 2011 R. 11.05 (2013).

[29] See Jennifer A. Leitch, 'Having A Say: "Access to Justice" as Democratic Participation', 4 *UCL J. of Law and Juris.* 76 (2015).

lawyers who must litigate against such people. Although the focus has tended to be on the mediative role and responsibilities of judges and decision makers in such contexts, there is a special burden on lawyers. Again, when dealing with the ethical dilemmas associated with litigation involving self-represented parties, it seems even more fruitful and sensible to deal with this as part of counsel's general duty to the court and the fair administration of justice.[30] As with many other matters, this will not work as a competing duty, but will serve as a check on lawyers' important duty to represent their own clients' interests in a forthright and loyal way.

Consequently, on the basis that any assistance given to an unrepresented opponent cannot be to the disadvantage of a lawyers' own client, a lawyer's responsibilities might fall short of some duty of candor to the opposing unrepresented party. It might still be demanded that lawyers take even more seriously their existing duty to ensure that all available information (e.g., case law, evidence, etc.) be placed before the court and that they only advance claims that are merit-based. This would also recommend that lawyers be doubly cautious to avoid undue legalese and to resist any excessive formalization of proceedings. Of course, lawyers must not ambush or deliberately create pitfalls for the unsophisticated and callow litigant; this general prohibition will be particularly exacting in dealing with self-represented litigants. Throughout, the underlying assumption is that the dynamics and performance of the lawyering contest have substantially changed because it can no longer be assumed that the other side knows the professional and implicit understandings of what it means to 'play the game' that are normally taken for granted when all litigants are lawyer-represented. Warriors are calculating and, at times, hard-hitting, but they are not bullies.

JUNIOR LAWYERS

As with most professional and collective enterprises, not all participants in the legal profession have equal authority. Some have the capacity and occasional responsibility to instruct other lawyers in

[30] *See, for example, Model Rules of Prof'l Conduct* R. 4.3 (2002); *CBA Code of Prof'l Conduct* ch. XIX, *Comm.* 8 (2009); *SRA Code of Conduct* 2011 R. 10, Guid. 2 (2013).

the way that they can and should perform their duties; this comes with the power to discipline those so instructed for their failure to act appropriately. With the growth of very large and hierarchically structured law firms, any code of ethical conduct ought, therefore, to give some consideration and weight to this 'chain of command' and its impact on lawyers' varying ethical statuses and expectations. Of course, military ethics has much to offer on this issue as the doctrine of 'superior orders' holds a significant place on its agenda of pressing matters. There are two related questions that pose themselves: Are individuals obliged to involve themselves in unjust wars (or pieces of litigation)? Must an individual always follow the orders of a superior officer (or lawyer)?

First, as regards participating in an unjust war, the principal position in military ethics is that the extent of a soldier's individual responsibility is based on the distinction between *jus in bello* and *jus ad bellum*. As such, soldiers are only to be held responsible for the justness of the actions that they commit during a war, while politicians and commanding generals are held responsible for the justice of the war itself. Nevertheless, there is the thorny question of what a soldier is supposed to do when asked to participate in a war that he or she does not think meets the established criteria for a just war.[31] There are two basic responses. The first and more mainstream view is that responsibility is proportionate to rank; only the highest-ranking officers need concern themselves about the justness of the war. This is based on the idea that rank-and-file soldiers have little autonomous choice once they sign up and take their military oath.[32] An alternative position is that, if soldiers are assumed to have a moral capacity, they

[31] *See supra* Chapter 6. I am leaving aside the broader issue of 'conscientious objection'. While this is an important topic in military matters, it tends to speak to the issue of whether one should become a lawyer at all rather than what one might do as a lawyer in a particular situation. *See* Fred C. Zacharias, 'The Lawyer as Conscientious Objector', 54 *Rutgers L. Rev.* 191 (2001). For a general discussion of 'superior orders' and an overview of the law, both Canadian and international, on this issue, *see* Leslie C. Green, 'Superior Orders and the Reasonable Man', in *Essays on the Modern Law of War* (2d ed. 1999); James Insco, 'Defense of Superior Orders Before Military Commissions', 13 *Duke. J. Comp. & Int'l L.* 389 (2003).

[32] *See* Walzer, *supra* note 12, at 22.

will be treated as capable of forming judgments about the justness of a war. However, even on this second view, allowance must be made for the fact that ordinary soldiers are in a limited position to question orders or have the necessary knowledge to make fully informed judgments; deference to authority is a realistic hedge on their moral responsibility.[33]

In the context of legal ethics, this reference to *ius ad bellum* has its equivalence in the selection of clients: What is the ethical responsibility of a junior lawyer instructed by a senior lawyer to work for a particular client or on a particular file? The distinction between the justness of the ends and the justness of the means seems to do reasonable work in the legal situation. Interestingly, the divided opinion among military ethicists plays out neatly in analyzing the dilemmas of junior lawyers.

While it will be different for single practitioners and even small firms, a junior lawyer is in no real position to determine or even influence the kind of clients and files that the larger law firms take on. While this fact will not relieve the junior lawyer of all professional responsibility, it will ease and diffuse the ethical pressure. Of course, it may well be that some lawyers will feel so strongly about the kinds of files that they are asked to work on or the kind of clients that the firm begins to take that they will feel morally compelled to seek a new job. This makes a junior lawyer's decision to join one law firm over another of even greater ethical import: the initial choice will set the stage for many other ensuing ethical challenges.[34] Accordingly, although all lawyers must take responsibility for the kind of general work they undertake and the kind of firm for which they work, they will not always be responsible for the justness of a particular client's cause or overall strategy. This dilemma is compounded by the fact that many young lawyers are burdened by educational debt and are trying to build a personal and family life.

Second, it is generally recognized that all soldiers are required to follow every order issued by a superior officer and to participate in

[33] *See* Jeff McMahan, 'The Ethics of Killing in War', 114 *Ethics* 693 (2004); David Estlund, 'On Following Orders in an Unjust War', 15 *J. Pol. Phil.* 213 (2007).

[34] *See supra* Chapter 6.

every conflict in which they are deployed. Consequently, this effectively relieves most military personnel from personal responsibility for their actions in so following orders. But there is a singular exception to this rule – 'manifest illegality'. Soldiers and officers not only can, but must refuse to obey any order that is transparently and clearly against domestic or international law; this includes taking action that would otherwise 'shock the conscience' of right-thinking people or would appear 'manifestly illegal' to a person of 'ordinary sense and understanding'.[35] Failure to reject such a manifestly unlawful order would make those soldiers and officers liable for committing an illegal act: the defense of deference to superior orders would not be available to them. This bifurcated doctrine of superior orders puts soldiers in something of an ethical bind as they are obliged to jump one way or the other. There is no room for any personal discretion or middle ground – obedience or disobedience is the order of the day. Moreover, there is little room or time for ethical debate in the immediate theater of war.

In the context of legal ethics, this doctrine of superior orders has limited, but important application. For instance, ABA Rule 5.2(b) states that lawyers should not be disciplined for their conduct as long as they were complying with "a supervisory lawyer's reasonable resolution of an arguable question of professional duty."[36] Apart from its vagueness, this rule parallels generally the superior orders defense in military ethics. Junior lawyers are afforded some leeway in agreeing to take actions that they might think are against the spirit of what counts as ethical lawyering. However, the room for maneuver is small as the junior lawyer must still be convinced that the supervisory lawyer's instructions are 'reasonable' and 'arguable': the onus is much more on junior lawyers than rank-and-file soldiers to think critically and accept some responsibility for their actions. While such a defense may be viewed as placing a chill on dissent and inculcating too deferential a response to

[35] *See, for example*, *Manual for Courts-Martial, United States* R. 916(d) (2012); Rome Statute of the International Criminal Court art. 33, July 17, 1998, U.N. Doc. A/CONF.183/9; 1 Queen's Regulations and Orders for the Canadian Armed Forces art. 19.015 n. C.

[36] *Model Rules of Prof'l Conduct* R. 5.2(b) (2002).

authority among junior lawyers, it does at least recognize some of the day-to-day realities of lawyering in large firms.[37]

Accordingly, while any reasonable evaluation of lawyers' ethical obligations must consider and be sensitive to existing power dynamics, it does not work to absolve them of all responsibility. There are moments when lawyers, like all persons, must speak truth to power. They must be prepared to stand and be counted, even if doing so results in personal loss and harm. Being an ethical lawyer, like being a good person, does not come without struggle and determination: it demands that principled conviction be put above personal interests. This is an exacting and onerous standard, but it is the honorable price to be paid for the privileges and prestige that come with being a professional lawyer. If private interests always eclipsed ethical considerations, this would relegate professional responsibility to an also-ran in the worthy and necessary ambition to play fairly. Legal ethics imposes burdens on lawyers in the name of the public interest. And that is how it should be.

CONCLUSION

In choosing to use just means to pursue just ends, it is important that lawyers do so in an ethical spirit of fair play. A legalistic attitude toward prevailing regulations and norms will lead some lawyers to view them as a ceiling rather than a floor: those lawyers will read back the rules of professional conduct and take the stance that anything that is not expressly prohibited is allowed. This pinched and formalistic perspective is the antithesis of an appropriate and honorable professional ethic. Because lawyers 'can' do something does not mean that they 'must' or

[37] Carol Rice, 'The Superior Orders Defense in Legal Ethics: Sending the Wrong Message to Young Lawyers', 32 *Wake Forest L. Rev.* 887 (1997); Andrew M. Perlman, 'Unethical Obedience by Subordinate Attorneys: Lessons from Social Psychology', 36 *Hofstra L. Rev.* 451 (2007). *See also* Andrew M. Perlman, 'The Silliest Rule of Professional Conduct: Model Rule 5.2(b)', 19 *Prof. Lawyer* 14 (2009). As Hazard contends, it is difficult to see how, if it is 'arguable', a supervisory lawyer could be disciplined. *See* Geoffrey C. Hazard & W. William Hodes, *The Law of Lawyering* § 43.5 (3d ed. 2001 & Supp. 2007).

even 'should' do it. A sober and genuine commitment to acting in a professional and ethical manner requires that lawyers challenge themselves to 'fight fair' in both letter and spirit. An ethical lawyer should be concerned to promote the reputation of the justice system and the legal profession; it is not enough simply to avoid bringing it into disrepute.

8

Toward a Just Peace

It seems to follow that, if there are strict conditions and guidelines for only waging just wars and with just means, there must also be attention given to ensuring that hostilities are ended and resolutions reached that are themselves in compliance with a set of just principles. The approval of settlements that are unjust and oppressive would make a mockery of any commitment to initiating and waging just wars and just litigation. As Michael Walzer puts it, 'implicit in the theory of just war is a theory of just peace.'[1] Accordingly, a sophisticated and rounded account of military ethics and legal ethics must set out parameters and principles for determining what counts as fair and reasonable outcomes after war and litigation ends. A just resolution of a conflict is the best way to avoid further wars and to ensure that peace is lasting.

COMING TO AN END

Although traditional practitioners of just war theory have been adamant about the need to wage just wars, and to do so only by just means, they have been relatively quiet about the ethical obligations that might be generated at or near the end of hostilities. They have tended to rest content with the ethical exhortation for military personnel and their civilian leaders to understand the ultimate ambition of a just war to be a lasting peace, not a temporary victory.

[1] Michael Walzer, 'Terrorism and Just War', 34 *Philosophia* 3, 4 (2006). *See also* A. J. Coates, *The Ethics of War* (1997); *The Price of Peace*, *supra* note 9.

However, there now exists a growing body of contemporary work on *ius post bellum*.[2] As with the requirements for just wars and just methods for waging them, the emphasis is on the kind of ethical principles that should guide behavior when one side triumphs over another. This covers matters like peace treaties, civilian reconstruction, war crimes trials and monetary reparations. As with most kinds of fair play, it is more important to be a good winner than good loser.

Not surprisingly, the ethical burden is placed squarely on the side of victors in their dealings with the vanquished – they must take all reasonable steps not to lord it over the losing side, especially by ensuring that the losing side is not able to participate as fully as possible in the international community of nations. In short, it is for the victor to be magnanimous and respectful in victory in order to garner ethical and professional approval and endorsement. Some of the more accepted principles include:[3]

(1) **Fair Termination of Hostilities** – A state may terminate a war if there has been a reasonable vindication of the rights that were initially violated and if the aggressor is willing to negotiate in good faith the terms of any surrender. These terms may include formal apologies, compensation, criminal prosecutions and rehabilitation. Alternatively, a state may end a war if it becomes clear that any just goals of the war cannot be reached at all or cannot be reached without using unjust means that will be excessive in the force used and the casualties suffered.

(2) **Rightful Intention** – A state may only terminate any war as long as its intention is to effect a reasonable peace that is in line with fair expectations and understandings. In particular, the vengeful settling of scores is to be avoided. As such, the victorious state must be willing to apply the same level of objectivity and scrutiny in prosecuting any war crimes its

[2] *See* Richard P. Dimeglio, 'The Evolution of the Just War Tradition: Defining Jus Post Bellum', 186 *Mil. L. Rev.* 116; Gary Bass, *Stay the Hand of Vengeance* (2001); Louis Iasiello, 'Jus Post Bellum: Moral Obligations of the Victors of War', 57 *Naval War College Rev.* 33 (2004).

[3] Brian Orend, *The Morality of War* (2006).

armed forces may have committed as it does against the vanquished state, especially if it was the initial aggressor.

(3) **Public Declaration** – The terms of peace must be negotiated and finalized between the designated representatives of the warring states' legitimate authority. Not only is the process of termination to be fair and just, but also the resulting agreement must be respectful of all parties' justifiable interests and rights on a going-forward basis.

(4) **Discriminate Treatment** – The victorious state must make suitable differentiations between political and military leaders, and combatants and civilians in determining their fate and responsibility for any immoral or illegal actions during the war. In particular, any punitive measures taken are to be confined to those directly responsible for the conflict. Although not obligatory, it is recommended that 'truth and reconciliation' should be given as much significance as the prosecution of war crimes.

(5) **Proportionality** – Any terms of surrender negotiated must be proportional to the rights that were initially violated. At the most basic level, there is to be no toleration for draconian measures, absolutist crusades and any similar attempt to deny the surrendered or vanquished state the right to reassume its participation in the world community.

Although work on this particular dimension of the just war tradition is more recent and, therefore, less developed, several helpful lessons can be drawn from it for the study of legal ethics and professional responsibility. As in the aftermath of war, important and seductive forces are in play that might encourage vengeful or retributive behavior on the part of the winning litigant. The most obvious parallel is with the ethics of negotiation and settlement; the ambition to do the best for one's client must be tempered and structured by the need to consider the impact on other parties. Accordingly, building on the basic duties that might be owed to opposing parties and non-parties during litigation,[4] it is instructive to consider how military ethics can inform the further development of legal ethics in regard to negotiating an end to ligation and hostilities generally.

[4] *See supra* Chapter 7.

BEYOND VICTORY

At the heart of the *ius post bellum* category is the foundational understanding that the abiding objective of entering and waging a just war is to achieve a just and lasting peace, not a punitive and temporary victory. Accordingly, the goal of military action is not simply to win, let alone to crush the enemy, but to work toward a future situation in which war will no longer be a possibility between the parties. It is considered that this cannot be achieved unless the victorious side negotiates a settlement that is fair and reasonable to both sides. In terms of military ethics, the principle of proportionality is accorded special significance – the substantive elements of any remedy achieved must be commensurate with the wrongful or transgressive conduct that gave rise to the hostilities in the first place.

This notion of a 'just peace' is distinctly lacking in most discussions of legal ethics and professional responsibility. The one area where it does seem to have some purchase is in the realm of criminal prosecution. It is generally agreed that the role of the prosecution is very different from that of defense counsel. Unlike their civil counterparts, prosecutors are more a part of the justice system and, as such, have a different set of ethical duties. Once charges have been laid, prosecutors assume sole carriage of the case. It is their responsibility to determine whether to continue with charges, whether to accept a plea bargain, what trial tactics to use, and whether to stay proceedings. In fulfilling this important task, the prosecutors are entrusted with the more public-oriented obligation not to seek convictions or exact severe punishment, but to remain neutral and even-handed. This means that they are not to be driven exclusively by the dictates and dynamics of winning and losing. Instead, prosecutors are expected to play the dual role of advocate and administrator– they must seek convictions for the guilty and, at the same time, guard against the wrongful convictions of the innocent. This translates into specific duties to put forward all credible and relevant evidence so that judge or jury can reach a just and warranted verdict and also to propose reasonable penalties at the end of a successful prosecution.[5]

[5] *See Model Rules of Prof'l Conduct* R. 3.8 (2002); and *CBA Code of Prof'l Conduct* ch. IX cmt. 9 (2009).

Perhaps the one area of litigation where the imperative of a just peace might have some important impact is that of family law. This is a notoriously difficult area of law in which passions run very high, the parties' willingness to act fairly is often attenuated, and the personal consequences can be enormous. The traditional and one-sided ethic of zealous advocacy for one's client points toward a less than balanced approach to terminating hostilities and reaching a reasonable compromise of interests. There is a tendency for lawyers to succumb to their clients' often righteous desire for revenge and to impose punitive conditions for settlement, especially in regard to child custody, support and related matters. There is little within the professional rules to invalidate such bellicose strategies; lawyers can easily assume a more mercenary-like and 'dogs of war' attitude in which they forego any responsibility to counsel clients of the benefits of striving for reasonable goals and acting reasonably toward the other party.

A greater respect for a just peace ideal and the incorporation of its facilitative principles might have salutary effects in family law matters. Rather than adopt a stance that might be more suited to litigation between strangers or corporate interests, lawyers might be empowered to work toward a compromise that allows both parties to establish fulfilling lives and, where appropriate, to enable a more harmonious family engagement. This would not mean that lawyers would assume the role of mediator or judge, but that they would pursue and defend their clients' interests with a more expansive ambition in mind. Instead of the client being the only focus of attention, there would be room to consider other interests, albeit in a secondary and looser form.[6] Such an approach might help to alleviate the tendency for parties to indulge in vengeful behavior, adopt draconian tactics and pursue short-term gains. More important, the ethical discourse around just peace might provide lawyers with useful resources to structure and direct their work.

BLUFFING AND CHEATING

Dissatisfaction with the adversary system by both lawyers and clients has led to a vast increase in alternative methods of dispute

[6] *Supra* chapter 7.

resolution. Although the shift from litigation to ADR is largely a function of society's desire for alternatives to lawyers and their adversarial mentality, it is inevitable that lawyers will continue to play a dominant role in the resolution of disputes. Of course, negotiation has always been a staple feature of most lawyers' practice: the wiles and ways of bargaining must be learned by all lawyers, exercised regularly and relied on extensively. However, the ethical landscape of negotiation is far from well-mapped or settled.[7] Consequently, there is ample room to explore the contribution that military ethics, especially the principles of *ius post bellum*, might make to a richer sense of lawyers' ethical responsibility in the practice of negotiation and bargaining.

Professional rules are very quiet on the ethics of negotiation; they tend to concentrate on advocacy matters. While there is a general exhortation to settle disputes on a reasonable basis and to avoid litigation for litigation's (or lawyers') sake,[8] there are no practical recommendations on how to perform such negotiations. The most that is required is that lawyers conduct themselves in an honorable way and that they advance their clients' interests without departing from the standard of 'honest dealing'.[9] Apart from these vague directives, lawyers are left to their own ethical sensibilities. However, there is a typical paucity of resources for lawyers to consult in addressing and resolving a whole slew of pressing issues in regard to negotiation: Does anything go? Or are there limits to what lawyers should be able to do on behalf of their clients? In particular, is it ever acceptable for lawyers to lie to gain the negotiating upper hand? Indeed, are lawyers ever required to lie for the good of their clients?

The traditional view of legal ethics does not encourage or countenance lying, but it does not outlaw it entirely. As part of the general traditional view to 'treat outsiders as if they were barbarians and enemies,' there are considered to be 'situations in which a lawyer

[7] For a nuanced and challenging inquiry into negotiation ethics, *see What's Fair: Ethics for Negotiators* (Carrie Menkel-Meadow & Michael Wheeler eds. 2004).

[8] *See Model Rules of Prof'l Conduct* R. 2.1 (2002); *CBA Code of Prof'l Conduct* chs. II, IX (2009); *SRA Code of Conduct* 2011 chs. 1, 11 (2013).

[9] *See Model Rules of Prof'l Conduct* pmbl. paras. 1–2. (2002); *See also CBA Code of Prof'l Conduct* ch. I (2009); *SRA Code of Conduct* 2011 Principles (2013).

may be duty bound to lie for his client'.[10] Some lawyers might well treat the negotiating table as one of those perverse locations in which lying is not only ethically justifiable, but might actually be morally mandated. The basic logic behind this uncompromising stand is that the role of lawyers is to act as champions, not moral consciences, for their clients. The prime ethical mandate is 'do what you can to help friend and harm enemy, as long as you stay within the law.'[11] If this requires lawyers to lie, then they should do so (as long as they are not under oath). The lie is not the lawyer's, but the system's; lawyers are actors in an institutional drama scripted by clients and society. Of course, many lawyers maintain that this approach is more compromised than uncompromising: the whole point of legal ethics is not to make lawyers the dupes for unscrupulous clients. That being said, it is also difficult to recommend that lawyers must at all times 'tell the truth, the whole truth, and nothing but the truth'.

Indeed, the ethical terrain of lying is rocky and demanding. Most people accept that telling a lie is not always immoral: much will depend on circumstances and consequences. For instance, telling lies to save lives seems not only excusable, but also desirable. Moreover, it is the rare lawyer who does not 'stretch the truth' in negotiations. The real problem is not simply whether it is ever acceptable for lawyers to lie in negotiating, but what are the types, limits and situations in which lawyers are entitled to engage in conduct that otherwise in non-lawyering situations might be considered not to be truth-telling. Without being pedantic or casuistic, it does seem that there is an important and defensible moral distinction between bluffing and lying, especially within a professional community and formalized setting. Lying involves not only telling untruths, but also doing so in order to mislead. In a context in which one professional negotiator is unlikely to accept all the other negotiator's statements at face value and is likely to be engaged in similar behavior, the dynamics and ethics of negotiation become contestable and unstable. Of course, if one party is self-represented, then this analysis might not apply so easily.[12]

[10] Charles Curtis, 'The Ethics of Advocacy', 4 *Stan. L. Rev.* 3 at 5 (1951).
[11] *Id.* at 7.
[12] *See supra* Chapter 7.

Perhaps the best answer to the issue of 'lying in negotiations' (and one that is highly recommended by military ethics) is that the negotiator's primary duty is to be fair and forward-looking. Obviously, some situations demand a high degree of integrity; this involves not lying about those matters that each lawyer thinks the other side would also not lie about. But it does not demand an absolutist commitment to always telling 'the whole truth and nothing but the truth'. Nevertheless, it is surely unethical to base any negotiated settlement on outright lies that undermine or compromise the whole basis for the settlement. Even if seasoned counsel represents the other side, it ought to be unprofessional, at best, both to advance unsubstantiated claims and to withhold significant facts. It might be one thing to keep quiet about certain matters, but it is another thing to connive in active misleading.

CONCLUSION

Ethical lawyers will work toward settlements that are reasonable and defensible. In some areas of law, this is achieved by requiring that settlements must be managed and approved by the courts.[13] However, even if such a requirement is not in place, there ought to be a genuine desire to reach a just outcome that will not depend on the other side's inexperience, weakness or negligent conduct; there is no honor in taking advantage of an adversary when they are already down and defeated. As with the litigation process itself, justice between the parties ought to be the abiding ambition of the system. Of course, the adoption of this standard can be very self-serving and allows all kinds of dubious conduct, but it seems the only sensible and reasonable solution. In both military and legal ethics, it is a paramount obligation to act both discriminately and proportionately. Indeed, it is the ethical signature of the warrior as opposed to the hired gun to be both a good winner and a good loser.

[13] A good example is class action litigation. In most jurisdictions, a settlement must be formally approved by a judge before it can be finalized and implemented. *See, for example, Federal Rules of Civil Procedure Rule 23 and 28 USCA §1332* (d) and *Class Proceedings Act s.29 1992 SO*.

9

Not-So-Final Thoughts

In this book, I have sought to demonstrate that the existing theory and practice of legal ethics and professional responsibility have been found seriously wanting. In both its traditional and contemporary forms, the deference of the standard model of legal ethics remains more of a threat to than a realization of a defensible account of ethical lawyering. Indeed, their message is doubly dangerous. Not only does it tend to perpetuate a style and substance of lawyering that can be very harmful to the public interest, but it also reassures lawyers that almost anything that they can do for their clients, no matter how dubious the clients' ends or how compromised the lawyers' motives or means, is ethical. Moreover, it is considered to be in the public interest as long as lawyers act within the narrow letter of the law. Such an approach is as intellectually bankrupt as it is morally debilitating.

By way of remediation, I have recommended that military ethics has substantial, if surprising potential to improve matters. It supplements and enriches the discursive resources that lawyers can use to address and occasionally resolve ethical challenges that perennially confront them. Instead of legal ethics being little more than a slightly upgraded distillation of contemporary lawyers' existing practices and established interests, it might fulfill its prime function of offering guidance to lawyers as to what is expected and occasionally required of them in certain situations. In particular, it can help lawyers to develop the moral sensitivity, moral judgment and moral conviction necessary to make a better and more ennobling job of fulfilling their professional role and responsibilities. Except for those who consider that both military ethics and legal ethics are irretrievably oxymoronic in title and substance, a mutual examination of each can be productive.

A CALL TO ETHICAL ARMS

As with any intellectual intervention, it is its practical merit that underwrites its theoretical validity. It is not difficult to float all manner of theoretical notions about legal ethics and professional responsibility. But it is a challenge of a different and more demanding order to do so and have a serious practical effect on the professional actions and ethical decisions of today's lawyers. The success of changing the way lawyers think about what they do must largely be measured by the extent to which it changes the way that lawyers do what they do. Insofar as this book has offered itself as a salvage exercise in the contemporary practice of legal ethics, it must be able to show the practical benefits of a different way of thinking about lawyers' professional responsibilities. Mindful that I have accepted certain foundational aspects of the existing legal process as a given (i.e., the adversarial system of litigation and the private economy of professional practice), I have explored the ways that the ideal of the ethical lawyer might be reimagined so as to advance better the best values and heightened ambitions of such a system.

In taking traditional scholars to task for their willingness to manufacture ever more novel explanations and justification for existing practices, I need to demonstrate that my reframing of lawyers' ethical duties by reference to military ethics will pay practical dividends and effect real changes. It is incumbent on my proposed alternative approach to offer the kind of ethical guidance and professional direction that will help lawyers in responding to some of the pressing dilemmas that they face in everyday legal practice. This is not to recommend that such dilemmas will simply disappear or lend themselves to easy resolution; they might actually increase. But it is to insist that my approach will offer genuine assistance in addressing and coping with them in a way that traditional approaches cannot and do not.

Consequently, I will end by putting traditional accounts of legal ethics and professional responsibility to the test by looking at two situations where lawyers are presented with difficult ethical dilemmas. As I have sought to show throughout, existing accounts and analyses seem to have nothing or little to contribute to their resolution. One situation involves the pleading of technical defenses and the other concerns the outer limits of confidentiality.[1]

The first situation is about a client (B) who is in financial straits and borrows $5,000 by way of a promissory note from his wealthy neighbor (L). L lets the note lapse. A number of years later, their financial situations are reversed and L feels obliged to seek the money back from B. For no apparent reason, B directs his lawyer to defend an action by L. The central question is whether B's lawyer should plead a solid limitation defense against the claim. In this scenario, there is considerable disagreement about what the lawyer should do and why; it is a classic problem that tends to divide many professional lawyers and legal ethicists.[2] The more traditional response is that, whatever the moral failings or motivations of clients, lawyers should not be troubled or tarred by such considerations: they not only can, but also should plead the limitations defense on behalf of B. Others may be less dogmatic. A bit like Tennyson's Light Brigade, lawyers are obliged to 'do or die':[3] they should comply or, if all else fails, withdraw from representing the client.

What joins these stronger and weaker traditional stances is that each has nothing to say about how to arrive at or make such a choice. For instance, the best that Bradley Wendel has to offer is that withdrawal should be 'a last resort'.[4] Most importantly, he (and other traditional theorists) suggests no discursive framework or set of resources through which the lawyer might be able to think about or determine what to do. Indeed, this gap or silence in the traditional position seems to be an almost necessary corollary of the prevailing 'hired gun' model – 'ask no questions and (maybe) tell no lies'. In recommending a sharp division between lawyers' personal and professional moral identities, the traditionalists divest

[1] *See supra* Chapter 3.

[2] *See, for example*, Stephen Pepper, 'Lawyers' Ethics in the Gap Between Law and Justice', 40 *S. Texas L. Rev.* 181 at 189–90 (1999) and Thomas Shaffer, 'The Legal Ethics of Radical Individualism', 65 *Texas L. Rev.* 963 at 977–9 (1987).

[3] Alfred, Lord Tennyson, 'The Charge of the Light Brigade' (1854). The actual quote is 'Theirs not to make reply,/ Theirs not to reason why,/ Theirs but to do and die.'

[4] W. Bradley Wendel, *Lawyers and Fidelity to Law* 128 (2010).

ethical lawyers of the tools and arguments that they might draw on in framing such questions, exploring available options and advancing possible answers.

While there is no easy or obvious answer to this professional quandary (and it would be silly to expect one), the worth of any ethical account is its ability to inform debate and structure available arguments. The alternative model of 'fighting fair' that I am suggesting has the distinct virtue and value of plugging this hole in traditional accounts of legal ethics. Looking at some of the moral precepts of 'just war' and 'just means', a number of important questions immediately spring to mind: Is there a distinction between what one 'can' and 'should' do? What are B's motivations for taking such a course of action? Is B a one-off client or is there a long-standing relationship? Are other local lawyers ready to take the case? How devastating will such a defense be to L's life? The traditional account has little to contribute to identifying, let alone addressing these and other pertinent questions. Instructed to leave their personal values and norms parked firmly at the door of their professional office, traditional lawyers are left to go it alone with no moral intuition or commitment to guide them. As Dante might have put it, 'Midway upon the journey of life,/ I found myself within a forest dark,/ For the straightforward pathway had been lost.'[5] What I have proposed may offer a more sustaining and helpful set of guidelines to move forward.

In addressing these questions within the richer normative milieu of a legal ethics infused with the spirit of military ethics, lawyers might be able to do much better. While it will not relieve them of the responsibility of deciding what to do, it will allow them to call on a nuanced range of ethical considerations that will inform their analysis and decision making. For instance, B's lawyer will want to ask if B is simply being bloody-minded or whether he has a more serious and sincere set of reasons for taking such an ostensibly unjust course of action; to inquire if there are other larger disputes between B and L; to weigh the consequences of taking such action and the impact on all parties, including L and other third parties; to be assured that all other avenues of settlement have been explored;

[5] Alighieri Dante, *The Divine Comedy*, c.1 (H. W. Longfellow trans., 1867).

and to assess B's chances of success. None of this is to say that B's lawyer must withdraw or that any lawyer who continues to represent B is somehow acting unethically. However, what this more substantive account of legal ethics and professional responsibility does is to oblige lawyers to address a more pressing series of interrogatories and also to furnish them with the some of the dialogic resources to work toward an answer to them.

PRIVATE VIRTUES, PUBLIC VICES?

The second example is the old chestnut of *Spaulding*.[6] Z's lawyer obtains a medical report on S that shows that S has an immediately life-threatening aneurism as a result of a car accident in which Z is at fault; S's own doctor missed this in his medical examination. Although the report is confidential, Z's lawyer has a duty to hand over the medical report, if asked by S's lawyer: no such request is forthcoming. The ethical dilemma is obvious: Can or should Z's lawyer voluntarily give the medical report to S's lawyer? If he does not, S will not be able to have the necessary life-saving surgery and might die. But, if he does, S's damages claim against his client Z will increase substantially.

Almost all commentators agree that Z's lawyers should have at least consulted with their client about whether to preserve confidentiality and that they should have urged the client to disclose.[7] However, there is sharp debate over what Z's lawyer should have done if Z insisted on keeping the information confidential and directly instructed the lawyer not to disclose it to anyone. After all, the failure to observe the life-threatening aneurism was a combination

[6] *Spaulding v. Zimmerman*, 116 N.W. 2nd 704 (Minnesota, 1962) and *supra* Chapter 3.

[7] *See, for example*, Roger Cramton and Lori Knowles, 'Professional Secrecy and Its Exceptions: Spaulding v. Zimmerman Revisited', 83 *Minn. L. Rev.* 63 (1998). Most rules of professional conduct impose a strict duty of confidentiality on lawyers and only allow disclosure where the lawyer strongly believes that the client intends to inflict serious harm on someone; *see Model Rules of Prof'l Conduct* R. 1.6 (b) (2002); *CBA Code of Prof'l Conduct* Ch. IV, Rule 4 (Can. 2009); *SRA Code of Conduct* 2011 Rule 4, Guid. 12–14, 18 (2013). Most commentators claim that this exception only applies in a criminal context and that it must be harm done by the client.

of S's own doctor's negligence on examining S and the negligence of his own lawyers in not asking for the medical report as they were fully entitled to do. Nevertheless, there are obviously strong countervailing reasons why a decision to breach confidentiality and ignore the client's direct instructions might be considered the ethical road to go down; saving a person's life seems to trump keeping secrets. While not quite Sophie's Choice, this is an ethical dilemma of the most excruciating professional kind.

Again, the traditional response is most revealing. For instance, Wendel concludes that 'I find the possibility of non-disclosure intolerable for moral reasons,... [so] the best course of action would be for his lawyer to disclose anyway and run the risk of professional discipline.'[8] Yet this seems to incorporate personal ethical reasoning, albeit of a noble kind, in exactly the way that the standard model being defended is designed to exclude. The main point of that traditional account of legal ethics is supposed to be that the ethical duty of lawyers is to 'subordinate' or 'exclude' ordinary moral concerns from their professional lives and 'as long as the lawyer acts within the law, her actions may not be evaluated in ordinary moral terms.'[9] This is a stark black-and-white world in which personal moral intuitions only seem to gain professional traction by stealth or subterfuge. Moreover (and again), traditionalists offer no reasoned basis or argumentative resources on which lawyers can rely in arriving at such decisions as professionals. In short, the traditional approach to professional responsibility is simply not up to the task of unpacking and confronting some of the compelling issues that might arise for the legal professional in search of ethical guidance.

In contrast, looking at some of the moral precepts of 'just war' and just means', a number of important questions immediately spring to mind – can or should Z's lawyer find an indirect way to tip off S's lawyer about his discovery rights? Can or should Z's lawyer find an indirect way to recommend that S be reexamined by the same or another doctor? How is the relative proportionality of the rights in play and the possible effects of exercising them to be

[8] Wendel, *supra*, note 4 at 75.
[9] *Id.* at 75, 155, 157 and 29.

considered? What pressure can or should be put on Z by the lawyer to 'do the right thing'? How might the interests of non-parties (e.g., S's family) be protected from the effects of any decision about what to do or not do? Should Z's lawyer, at least, refuse to be part of such a course of action by the client? These questions have the benefit of both focusing lawyers' ethical attention and giving them a more helpful way to think about them.

Again, none of this is to say that Z's lawyer must withdraw or that any lawyer who continues to represent Z is necessarily acting badly or unprofessionally. Whichever way the lawyer turns (i.e., preserve confidentiality in this instance because it will serve the public interest in the long term or break the confidentiality because it promotes the public interest in this instance), she or he will be open to both praise and criticism from professional colleagues and laypersons alike. In an important sense, the lawyer is perhaps hostage to a bad rule that might be revised to include an exception for the circumstances in *Spaulding*'s case. Indeed, one ethical response is to approach the law society with a view to changing the confidentiality rule in civil cases to provide a more even and public-spirited balance of competing interests.[10]

However, a more substantive and nuanced account of legal ethics and professional responsibility (as suggested and supplemented by military ethics) does oblige lawyers to address a more pertinent series of interrogatories and furnishes them with a more sophisticated set of dialogic resources to confront them. No formulaic or straightforward conclusions will easily recommend themselves, especially in genuinely hard cases like *Spaulding*. Although lawyers will still have to possess the moral conviction and self-discipline to follow through on the decided-upon moral course of action, the process of ethical judgment and decision making will have been enriched and deepened. And that is no small achievement in the existing rudimentary world of legal ethics and professional responsibility.

[10] There is a continuing debate over whether the confidentiality rules serve more the material interests of lawyers than the public interest; they are able to commodify this benefit and increase the demand for their services. *See, for example*, W. H. Simon, *The Practice of Justice: A Theory of Lawyers' Ethics* (1998) and Daniel Fischel, 'Lawyers and Confidentiality', 65 *U.Chi L. Rev.* 1 (1998).

CONCLUSION

The central and connecting theme of this book has been the need to impress upon lawyers that they are part of a justice system, not only a legal process. They are accorded the privileges and power that they have on the condition that they assume duties and responsibilities that serve the public interest; this is different from satisfying people's private interests, including and especially their own, or from the public interest being merely the sum of private interests. In an adversarial age, lawyers can still fulfill their professional duties with fairness and justice. It is not so much that lawyers must be adversaries that is the central problematic, but more how lawyers can be adversaries and still meet a high standard of ethical behavior. By abandoning the role of hired guns and thinking of themselves as honorable warriors, lawyers can develop a mentality and pattern of conduct that is more conducive to achieving an ethical and proud standard of professional esteem. By so doing, lawyers will not only advance better the social cause of justice, but also enhance the reputation of their profession.

While there are no last words that can or should be said about the theory and practice of legal ethics and professional responsibility, a fitting place to bring this book to a close is with the stirring words of President Barack Obama. In his acceptance speech on being awarded the 2009 Nobel Peace Prize, he threw down a challenge to political and military leaders in thinking about 'just war'. This compassionate plea is as urgent and as compelling for lawyers in their professional undertakings as anybody else. In a small way, I hope that this book has made a modest contribution to the task of obliging lawyers to live up to their ethical calling and of making them a more responsible profession:

> I do not bring with me today a definitive solution to the problems of war. What I do know is that meeting these challenges will require the same vision, hard work, and persistence of those men and women who acted so boldly decades ago. And it will require us to think in new ways about the notions of just war and the imperatives of a just peace.[11]

[11] Barack Obama, President of the United States, Remarks by the President at the Acceptance of the Nobel Peace Prize, December 10, 2009, http://www.whitehouse.gov/the-press-office/remarks-president-acceptance-nobel-peace-prize.

Index

For EU product safety concerns, contact us at Calle de José Abascal, 56–1°, 28003 Madrid, Spain or eugpsr@cambridge.org.

www.ingramcontent.com/pod-product-compliance
Lightning Source LLC
La Vergne TN
LVHW011513200926
848484LV00001B/28
* 9 7 8 1 1 0 7 1 1 6 9 1 7 *